AN AMERICAN PROCEEDING

AN AMERICAN PROCEEDING

Building the Grant House with Frank Lloyd Wright

Donna Grant Reilly

Meadowside Press
HANOVER, NEW HAMPSHIRE

DISTRIBUTED BY
UNIVERSITY PRESS OF NEW ENGLAND
HANOVER AND LONDON

Distributed by

University Press of New England

1 Court Street, Suite 250, Lebanon NH 03766

Manufactured in the United States of America

ISBN: 978-1-58465-978-5

Library of Congress Number: 2010900873

For Doug and Jackie Grant

CONTENTS

ACKNOWLEDGMENTS

It would have been almost impossible for me to write *An American Proceeding* without the help of my brother, David Grant. He spent many hours searching through the family collection of photographs; he dug out old records, checked facts and researched long-forgotten details. He corrected me when I got things wrong, and spent many hours conferring with me about events we each recalled a little differently. I can never thank him enough.

My sincere gratitude goes to Bruce Brooks Pfeiffer, at the Wright Foundation, for giving me the impetus I needed to start this book. His assistance, encouragement and generosity have been greatly appreciated.

My thanks go to Pat Tracy for preserving and re-formatting the taped interviews I made with my parents in the late '70s. Although most of the photos in the book come from the Grant family collection, I would like to thank Phil Feddersen for giving me permission to use some of the photos he took during construction. I am particularly grateful to Jack Barrett and Mark Polizzotti for the help and encouragement they gave me during the entire process.

Finally, I could not have done any of this without the support of my husband, Chuck Reilly. He gave me encouragement, thoughtful criticism and helpful suggestions; he must have read the manuscript a dozen times. What is more, he gave me the time I needed and the self-confidence I sometimes lost sight of. And even though I spent many hours in front of the computer, neglecting everything except this book, he continued to give me the time and space I needed to see it through to the end.

FOREWORD

THE DOUGLAS GRANT HOUSE

"I believe a house is more a home by being a work of art."
—Frank Lloyd Wright, *The Natural House*, 1954

At the entry on the upper level, to descend inside the long stairway enclosed by massive native stone walls on either side, to the two story living room below, is to lead you into a world of medieval romance, as though you are in a twelfth century French castle, down to a world of present day splendor, into a living room where three walls of glass, fifteen feet tall, reveal to you all the glories of nature in its ever-changing seasons. This is the house that Frank Lloyd Wright designed for Jackie and Douglas Grant.

The most remarkable thing about this house is that it was built, for the most part, by the Grants themselves. Douglas Grant acted as the general contractor, and when a stage of construction was new to him, he sought out books and journals that would teach him the craft and techniques that he needed to go on building. Jackie Grant was on the site from the very beginning in the role of a construction worker, at the same time managing a household and raising three children. Their daughter, Donna, has written an intense account of how this all took place.

"This is an American proceeding, building their own house", as Wright described what the Grants had heroically undertaken while the house was still in construction, "And they certainly ought to have a house. They're all tumbled up in a pile with three children, and the parents, but they're getting a lot of fun out of that house, I know. It is going to be beautiful...The chimney's finished, and the second story is poured, and now he's busy bending the conduit and putting it in the walls and floors himself. He's no electrician, never had done anything of that kind before. He's a radio man, a very bright fellow. If every G.I. had the wit and intelligence to go ahead and build a house the way he's building his, our colleges would be greatly relieved. Yes, pleasing, astonishing to see what he has done." *

The journey that the Grants undertook to turn Wright's drawings into a home of their own was fraught with hardships, anguish, and often heart-breaking difficulties. There were problems and disappointments. However, the Grant house ranks among some of the finest and most inspired homes that Frank Lloyd Wright ever designed. Here is a home for the average American family of moderate means. It is in that genre of homes that Wright called "Usonian"—a building for a family in the United States, wherein beauty and repose is possible without ostentation or great wealth. The greater amount of his work was residential, and of his residential work, the greater part of that category was the many homes he designed for middle-income families, such as the Grants. Further, of those homes, this one rightfully takes a special place, unique in Wright's work, due to the design with its companionship to the landscape and the fact that it was primarily built by the clients themselves with much hard work all along the way, but with much determination and devotion.

BRUCE BROOKS PFEIFFER, Director of Archives
Frank Lloyd Wright Foundation
Taliesin West, November 22, 2007

* Frank Lloyd Wright to the Taliesin Fellowship, 1958

PREFACE

Throughout the literature on Frank Lloyd Wright and his architecture one finds many stories about the people who lived in the houses he designed for them. Nearly all of them considered it a rare privilege to be among the fortunate number who achieved that distinction.

But there was an even more select group of Wright homeowners, rarely mentioned in any of the literature: a small band of men and women who built their Frank Lloyd Wright homes from the ground up—doing all or most of the work themselves—and who were largely unaware of each other. In most cases they had some building experience, and often it was the only way they could afford to build. Apparently, Wright fully approved of these endeavors, once he was satisfied that the job would be done to his satisfaction. The idea of a man building his own house was pleasing to Wright; he liked to tell his clients about the virtues of hard work and how a little sweat would help them to appreciate their house even more.

There isn't much written about the people who built their Wright designed houses with little or no outside help. Most, if not all of them, are gone, and we may never know the full story of how they coped with the experiences they encountered as a result of choosing to build on their own. In 1946, Frank Lloyd Wright designed a house for my parents—Mr. and Mrs. Douglas Grant—in Cedar Rapids, Iowa. My parents not only did most of the construction themselves, but they quarried the stone that went into the walls. The work was hard and it took them a long time, but their reward was the unique distinction of living in a Wright design to which they had given form.

Wright was also fond of telling his clients that living in one of his houses would change their lives—a dramatic statement indeed. But his prediction was one worthy of the Oracle at Delphi; at the time, one didn't stop to wonder if that change would be for better or for worse!

The story of how my parents built their Frank Lloyd Wright house is a remarkable one. I was there when it happened, and I remember it very well. I'd like to share it with you.

DONNA GRANT REILLY, March 2010

AN AMERICAN PROCEEDING

Jackie and Doug Grant, 1931

A Desire to Get Away

It was still dark outside when Dad woke us up. We got out of bed quickly, put on the clothes that Mother had laid out for us the night before and hurried downstairs to breakfast. It was a Saturday morning in October 1946; I was eleven and my brother, David, was six. We didn't know we were about to set off on a journey that would substantially change our lives but, even though we were still very young, we sensed that this would be no ordinary trip in the car. This time we were going to a place called Spring Green, Wisconsin and we were going to meet Frank Lloyd Wright.

It wasn't as if Mother and Dad had always wanted a Frank Lloyd Wright house; in fact they had never heard of Wright much before 1945. But, once they had decided upon the perfect spot for their new house, they realized they were going to need help finding the right kind of house to put there. More importantly, they knew they would never be able to afford the house they wanted unless they built it themselves. They needed to find an architect who was willing to work with them on those terms.

They built their first house in 1936, a compact little brown-shingled bungalow that settled in comfortably between a dense woods and a big rolling pasture on the outskirts of Cedar Rapids, Iowa. A desire to get away from the city, combined with a strong determination to bring up their children with all the advantages of exposure to fresh air, grass and trees, made it possible for them to overlook the fact that they didn't have much money. Dad was an announcer and news man for radio station KWCR at the time, and they were living in a tiny rented house in the Kenwood section of Cedar Rapids.

Doug Grant was a city boy. He was born in 1908 in St. Paul, Minnesota and lived there until he was twelve, when his parents moved to Des Moines, Iowa. He was the eldest of four children—all boys. In keeping with their Scottish surname, Ruth and Willis Grant named their boys Douglas, Donald, Bruce and Robert. The household was a lively one and, since their father was ten years older than their mother and didn't have much of a sense of humor, the boys frequently provoked him into losing his temper. When I was growing up, I knew that Grandpa Grant worked for the Iowa State Department of Rehabilitation, but it never occurred to me to ask anybody what that meant. In the 1940's Grandma became the editor of *The Rehabilitation Journal*. I didn't really know what that was either, but I remember lots of pictures of wheel chairs and artificial limbs. Maybe it wasn't the most exciting of all jobs, but it was unusual for a woman in those times to have a job outside the home at all. Grandma Grant, a great beauty in her youth, had a passionate love for music and believed that everyone would be better off if they made music a part of their lives. I suppose Dad's love of music started that way; he loved it all his life. Another gift he surely acquired from his mother was the strong desire to learn. He read voraciously until the last years of his life, and he truly believed that you could learn anything if you read enough about it. Although it was financially difficult for his parents to send him to college, he began with a scholarship in vocal music at Oberlin College and, later, another one to Drake University in Des Moines. It was there he met another vocal music student named Jackie Kinkead.

Charlotte Jaquetta Kinkead (she hated the name Charlotte, and was always called "Jackie") was born in 1909, the youngest daughter of George and Caroline Kinkead. She and her six siblings were born and raised on a farm near Rippey, Iowa—one of the small communities that dot the rich farming land around Des Moines. Her people were farmers who were familiar with the close relationship between man and nature, and who followed a long tradition of hard work without much expectation of reward. When Mother was thirteen, her mother died of a sinus infection. Her father drifted away from home shortly after, apparently consumed by grief and depression, but not before he had placed his two youngest children in the care of their older, married siblings. Mother went to live with her oldest sister, Polly, a strict taskmaster who had little time for the affection that a young girl needed after losing both parents. But in the 1920's, life was often hard on a farm, and it couldn't have been easy for Aunt Polly and Uncle Fred to take in another child; they had three children of their own. Mother was expected to work hard for her keep, but she loved to sing and it was to become her salvation. She managed to win a music scholarship in 1928 to Drake University, in Des Moines, and a job working as a live-in nanny to her voice teacher's only child.

Mother and Dad met in Des Moines while they were both attending Drake and singing in the choir at Plymouth Congregational Church. During those years before the Great Depression, attending college was an expensive privilege for middle-class Americans. Many were having difficulty just finding a job. But it soon became obvious to the Grant family that Dad was very much in love with Mother and they wanted to get married. Grandpa took Dad aside and said to him,

"Your mother and I both think you and Jackie should get married, but we can't afford to continue paying for college if you do. You'll have to choose which you want most and, if you decide the way I think you will, you'll have to go to work to support your new wife."

Mother and Dad were married at Plymouth Congregational Church on June 16, 1931, during a summer of record-breaking heat. For their honeymoon, they drove to Colorado and spent a week camping and climbing Pike's Peak.

Now that they were no longer attending college, they needed to find employment. Dad worked any job he could find, but he had an interest in the new business of radio broadcasting and managed to get some experience working at a local station in Des Moines. Mother was one of the few women lucky enough to have a job during those difficult years; most women were told that jobs would go to men because they needed to support their families. She worked as a sales clerk in the sheet music department of the Des Moines Music Store, her music training considered an asset by her boss. That she was young and attractive was undoubtedly an asset as well. By a stroke of good luck, the Des Moines Register and Tribune, Iowa's leading newspaper, acquired a small radio station in Ottumwa, Iowa and Dad was sent there to help run it. So Mother lost her job, but Dad gained a leg-up in the broadcast business which became his life's career. They stayed in Ottumwa for two years until 1934, when Dad got a job with radio station KWCR (later to become WMT) in Cedar Rapids. I was born a year later.

On nice weekends, we all set off in the car to explore the countryside beyond the edge of town. One spot in particular had become a favorite, and we went there often to relax and breathe the cool fresh air. It could only be reached by driving to the top of an extremely steep hill, turning onto an obscure dirt road which soon stopped altogether, then abandoning the car and hiking the rest of the way in. The reward was a majestic panoramic view across a deep valley with a creek curving along below. There were rolling meadows and wooded hillsides as far as one could see, and the cool green was welcome refreshment after the hot, sticky pavement of town. There were only two houses on the entire "street"; it was a wonderful spot for a house and, although that idea seemed quite remote at this point, there was no harm in asking who owned the land. Dad made inquiries at the courthouse and learned that two small lots on the site belonged to Mrs. Rosa Rider, a widow living in the neighboring town of Marion. Mrs. Rider's husband had been a grocer who acquired the two lots, each measuring roughly 40 feet by 200 feet, as payment for an outstanding grocery bill. After thorough consideration of the matter, Mrs. Rider agreed to sell the lots for $50 each—probably the amount of the original debt. It was a bargain, even for those days, and Mother and Dad were elated, even though they were $100 poorer. Not only was the newly-purchased land a bargain, but it was secluded and likely to remain that way. The surrounding acres to the north, east and west were owned by the county. The land had originally been intended for the county old peoples' home, but another site was chosen for that purpose. This land lay unused and apparently forgotten, so Mother and Dad felt they had a virtual guarantee that their beloved view would remain unspoiled.

Now that the little plot of land was theirs, Mother and Dad began to think seriously about building on it. They settled on the idea of a summer cottage—a place to escape to during the hot summer months in town. They figured they could put together a modest structure with no plumbing, heating or basement for very little money if they did all the work themselves. A fireplace was a major requirement, however; and if necessary they would begin with that and gradually build the cottage around it, as they could afford to do so. One evening, at a friend's house, they met a young, local builder/architect named Bruce McKay, who was beginning to enjoy a certain amount of success designing residences. As they talked excitedly about their new land and the plans they had for building on it, he became quite interested, finally saying, "I'd like to design it for you."

"Oh, we can't afford to pay an architect," they protested.

"That's all right. I'd like to do it just for the fun of it," he insisted. He felt strongly, however, that they should plan for at least a partial basement to accommodate a furnace so they would have the option of using the house in colder weather, as well. In the next few months the suggestions and changes grew so numerous that they soon realized their summer cottage had become a permanent home. The plans for the little house were exquisite; after all, Bruce McKay customarily designed large, expensive homes for the wealthier citizens of Cedar Rapids. He enjoyed designing this little house and began calling it "The Playhouse".

Playhouse or not, it now had to be built and paid for. In the summer of 1936, Mother and Dad obtained a loan on their insurance policy to finance the building materials, and they began their education in the building of houses. A few years before his death, I asked Dad why he thought he could build a house when he'd had no experience doing anything of the kind. His answer was simply,

"I always figured that if carpenters, electricians and plumbers could learn to do those things, I could learn them, too."

He was right, of course. First he read everything he could find on the subject and then he talked to those who did it for a living. They hired a neighbor to extend the road down to the building site and to dig out the basement and foundations—which he did with a shovel for 50 cents an hour. They hired a carpenter to help with the framing, and the rest they did themselves, with some valuable assistance from Grandpa Grant, an accomplished handyman.

At this point, Dad was working at the radio station from nine to five on weekdays and nine to noon on Saturdays. At one time he also had a weekly Sunday morning program called "The Gospel Baritone", which consisted mostly of Dad singing hymns, as far as I can remember. There was also a period when he and Mother read aloud the comic pages over the radio on Sunday morning—Dad did all the male characters and Mother did the females. Most of the remaining time was devoted to building the house. As soon as the house was framed in, they built a rough playpen for me so that Mother could work without worrying about where I was. Nevertheless, I'm told that I became quite good at calling her down from the rafters on one pretext or another, and I overturned nail cans whenever they were placed too close to the bars of my "cage". Well into my adult life, Mother still insisted on telling anyone who would listen that I seasoned all of the floors in that house by peeing on them.

I believe Mother had her first taste of women's equality when she became a builder. The workmen who helped with the house soon took her presence for granted and she was almost "one of the boys". Mother and Dad had installed a telephone at the house so they could communicate while Dad was at the radio station. Mother finished a telephone consultation one afternoon, rushed over to scoop up her can of nails and went sprawling across the floor to an accompaniment of thigh-slapping laughter. The well drillers had just pulled an old carpenters' joke on her by nailing her can of nails to the floor. Equality sometimes has its price.

As soon as they had a well, life became a little easier; now they at least had water, even if there was no plumbing yet. That summer, the temperature reached 113 degrees. Mother and Dad rose before dawn so we could escape to the building site where it was somewhat cooler. This way, Dad could devote a few hours to building before going to work. When his morning construction work ended, Dad took a shower by having Mother hose him down before he dressed for the office. They were surrounded by woods, and there were no nearby neighbors, but the water from the well must have been pretty cold! Plumbing was installed in a short time, however, and Grandpa Grant was a great help here. Dad had never before seen anyone do a leaded joint; Grandpa had seen it done once. Between them they figured it out, each added a new skill to his repertoire and we now had a toilet.

The Grant family moved into their partially finished, self-built house in early fall of 1936. Mother and Dad had been invited to a dinner party that night by one of the town's most influential citizens, and they saw no reason to pass up the invitation. Hiring the carpenter's sister to stay with me at the new house, they spent their last moments in the old house in Kenwood bathing and changing from scruffy work clothes into party finery. That done, they tossed their work clothes into the back seat, said goodbye forever to city dwelling and went off to dine in style.

Moving is never fun, but moving into a house that you have built yourself, and not yet finished, is a major undertaking. Of course they never dreamed they would be doing it again in fifteen years—and on a much larger scale.

TWO

A Beautiful Parcel of Land

As the years went by, the Grant family grew; my brother, David, was born in December 1939 and my sister, Linda, in January 1942. The two bedroom, one bathroom "Playhouse" was beginning to get a little crowded. Dad finished the attic to make bedrooms for the three children, which was not a difficult job for him. The difficulty came when it was time to figure out how to get us up there. A ladder up through the trap door to the attic was greeted with enthusiasm by the three of us, but was voted down as too impractical. There was very little space for a stairway; it would have to be a winding staircase, and Dad had never built one of those. Recognizing his limitations, he interviewed a local handyman, Mr. Firemartin, who assured Dad that he had vast experience with staircases and was the man for the job. Dad took him at his word and Mr. Firemartin started the next week.

It soon became apparent, however, that the job was taking Mr. Firemartin much longer than he had indicated. He seemed to be ripping out as much as he was building, and the whole process was accompanied by streams of invective. Mother began sending us out to play when Mr.

Firemartin was working, but it was obvious that the job was not going well. Finally, after a particularly frustrating day, he told Mother that he had a bad headache and was going home. When Dad called him the next day to find out how he was feeling, Mr. Firemartin said,

"My head still aches pretty bad. I don't know when I'll be able to get back to the job."

Dad had a reasonably good idea of what the real trouble was, so he said, "I might be able to finish up the stairs by myself. Would that be all right with you?"

"Oh, yes," came the relieved answer. "That'd be fine with me."

Dad had no choice but to do it himself. So, using his time-honored method, he went looking for books on how to build a staircase. After much study, and a lot of work with pencil, paper and slide-rule, he started in. I don't remember how long it took him to do it, but he got that staircase built. It was very steep, and would probably not win any prizes for design; but it went up to the attic and it came down, and that was what we needed.

As the years went by, the little street where we lived was discovered by others and more houses were built there. Mother and Dad began to question their original premise that the county-owned land beyond them would always be vacant. The thought that this beautiful parcel of land, one they had almost begun to think of as theirs, could be developed and built on by others was not comforting at all. Dad went to talk to the appropriate person at the county offices and inquired about the possibility that the land might be for sale. The consensus was that no one had thought about that property for years, but if Dad cared to make them an offer for it, someone would consider it. After much consultation with Mother, and a realistic look at the budget, Dad made a formal offer for the 47.5 acres of land at a price of $50 an acre.

He didn't hear anything from them for months and was beginning to think that, either it had become lost on someone's desk or was considered too low a bid to even consider. At that time, we were spending a week or two each summer at a little cabin on a lake in Minnesota during Dad's vacations from the radio station. The cabin was owned by a family friend who didn't use it much any more and, finally, Dad offered to buy it from her. He had just made a down-payment when he received a letter from the county. They had accepted his bid and, if he was still interested, the land was his. Hallelujah! But wait—the cabin in Minnesota. Fortunately, the down-payment on the cabin was returned, and they were once again able to obtain a loan on their insurance policy. And so, on July 25, 1941, the 47.5 acres became the property of Mr. and Mrs. Douglas Grant. From that time on, our lives would never be the same.

It is a beautiful piece of land, and at that time it was a large expanse of rolling pasture land surrounded by woodlands. Some of it was planted in corn by an old farmer who used mules to do his plowing, and later it was used to graze a few milk cows belonging to a Czechoslovakian family named Rudish who lived nearby. The land sloped down to a wide valley below with Indian Creek running through it, serving as the Grant property boundary on the west. There was one spot in particular: a grassy point of land, jutting out to the west, which dropped off gradually on three sides and afforded a panoramic view of the countryside in three directions. We all began referring to that area as "The Point", and we loved to go there and just sit for a while. In clear weather you could see for miles, and at night the lights of Cedar Rapids and the neighboring town of Marion seemed insignificant when compared to the spectacular view of the stars overhead. Sometimes, on winter nights, we would have a rare display of aurora borealis, a light show so magnificent you would swear you could hear it. It was the place where we often played children's games, where our family had picnics, and where Mother and Dad went to dream about the house they would build there some day.

Once the land was ours, exploring it took on a new dimension. My brother and I ran through the woods, picking wild flowers in the spring and playing in the streams caused by the melting snow; wading in the creek on hot summer days; swinging on grape vines and jumping off into enormous piles of leaves in the fall; and sledding in the winter until the cold numbed our hands and feet, finally driving us indoors to warm them up again.

Mother and Dad were excited by all the trees we had acquired, but even more exciting was the discovery of an abandoned limestone quarry down in the creek bottom land. After making some inquiries, Dad learned that there had, indeed, been a working quarry there many years ago, but what people remembered most was that the quarry was also the site of the locally famous "Horse Thief Cave". The cave was at one time the entrance to a vast labyrinth of caverns that ran back into the surrounding countryside and no doubt still do. It was reputed to have been a way-point for bands of horse thieves who frequented the area many years ago, serving as a convenient hiding place for the stolen horses they ran from one county to the next. In the late 1800's, as local lore had it, a group of spelunkers (or a small boy, depending on which version you got) who were exploring the caverns became lost within the maze of passages below and were never found. As a result, the cave was considered a danger to all and was blasted shut by the county, preventing any further exploration. There are, however, people who never give up and, by the time my parents bought the property, it was obvious that attempts had been made to reopen the cave. It must have taken an impressive amount of digging to open up the hole that we discovered; it was only about ten or twelve inches in diameter, but big enough for a skinny kid to wriggle through. No one likes the idea of an "attractive nuisance" on his property and Dad was no exception. He spent a long time working to block the hole with large stones that would at least serve as a deterrent until he could close it more permanently. Nevertheless, David and I enjoyed a certain degree of celebrity at school when it became common knowledge that we owned "Horse Thief Cave".

Although grass, weeds and even trees had grown over the face of the old quarry, there was enough of the stone visible for Mother and Dad to see that it was quite attractive. It was then that they began thinking about their stone as possible building material for a future house. When they began cleaning away some of the vegetation obscuring the stone, they could see that it formed very distinctive strata, which appeared to be of varying thickness. As they began prying out some of the stone, they discovered that it came out rather easily and, once the stone was exposed, it proved to be extremely hard, breaking into pieces with sharp, jagged edges and producing a ringing tone when struck with a hammer. This, in itself, was unusual, since most of the limestone found locally was much softer. This would also prove to be a matter of some frustration and concern in the months ahead. For now, however, the more rock they dug out the more excited they became. There appeared to be two colors here—a light gray with almost pink overtones and a slightly darker shade of tan, both types containing generous pockets of quartz crystals. All of it was beautiful and it looked like there was plenty more where that came from. They brought up enough to build a small stoop at the front door of our little brown house and a stone walk out to the street.

I don't know just when they began to talk about building a house on this property. They knew exactly where it would go, because they had talked for years about building on The Point some day. Now they were excited about the possibility of building with timber from their own land and limestone from their quarry. They had talked often about what kind of house they wanted, and both believed it was important to have a house that was visually compatible with the surrounding landscape. They also knew that, whatever kind of house they decided on, they would have to build most of it themselves. They had built the little brown house and, although they had needed help from others along the way, they were sure they could do it again. Did they realize then that the next house would undoubtedly be a much greater project than any they had tackled in the

past? I don't know, but I do know they were young, healthy and determined to let nothing discourage them from having the house of their
dreams. Planning for their house, even if it had no substance yet, excited
them; just talking about it made it seem closer to reality.

But it would have to wait. On December 7, 1941, the Japanese attacked
Pearl Harbor. The country was at war, and all planning came to a sudden
halt.

THREE

Whatever Consideration You Can Give

In 1938, *Architectural Forum* magazine devoted the entire issue to the work of Frank Lloyd Wright. Dad and Mother spent a lot of time looking at photos of houses, trying to find a style that appealed to them, but Dad kept returning to that 1938 magazine with Frank Lloyd Wright's work. Chicago was not very far away and neither was Wright's home near Spring Green, Wisconsin, but his work was not widely known in eastern Iowa at that time. Those who had heard of Wright at all were more familiar with the well-publicized circumstances of his personal life than they were with his architecture. I don't think Dad knew much of anything about Frank Lloyd Wright's work until he came across that issue of the Forum at the local library. Evidently he was successful in purchasing a copy of the magazine, and he read it thoroughly many times; Wright's work appealed to him, and he had never seen anything like it. Now, going over it again in 1945, Mother and Dad still thought there was something unique and wonderful about the way Wright's houses fit into their surroundings. They were particularly impressed by the photos of Taliesin, Wright's home in Wisconsin. It was made of stone that appeared to be much like the stone in our quarry, and the rolling Wisconsin countryside where it was located resembled that of eastern Iowa. After discussing it at length with Mother, Dad decided to go ahead and approach Wright. The worst that could happen was that he would say no. So, on December 26, 1945, Dad wrote to Frank Lloyd Wright:

"Dear Mr. Wright:

"I have owned a copy of the January 1938 *Architectural Forum* … ever since it was published. During that time I have read and re-read it many times, hoping that the day would arrive when our family might actually build a home as admirably suited to our needs and location as the houses in that magazine.

"Now the time has come when we dare to begin thinking actively of building such a home. Would it be possible for you to design it for us? If you are unable to do it personally could you suggest an architect who is capable of carrying on the ideas and ideals you have established?

"We are fortunate in owning a tract of 50 acres of hilly land on the outskirts of Cedar Rapids. We have set aside one of the hilltops for our future home site. The tract also includes some heavily wooded areas and an abandoned stone quarry. We have talked with local builders about the possibility of working into our house native lumber from our trees and stone from our quarry. None of them pretends to know anything about such heresy but all are quite sure it isn't practical.

"Our family consists of Mrs. Grant and me, two daughters, ten and four, and a son, six. Because of our family's size, we would like to have four bedrooms. We can afford to spend between $10,000 and $12,000 for our new home. We realize that building costs have increased considerably in recent years and that perhaps we can't build a four-bedroom home for that price. On the other hand, we are hopeful that a skilled architect, by carefully utilizing the materials at hand, and by eliminating unnecessary expenditures, may be able to give us what we need and remain within the budget.

"Whatever consideration you can give our project will be appreciated sincerely.

Yours very truly,

Douglas B. Grant"

Grant children: Linda, Donna and David, ca. 1945

In reviewing the letter today, I am struck by how skillfully it was designed to accomplish its purpose. It begins by paying tribute to Wright and his work, and then gets right to the point by asking him to design the house. When Dad suggests that Wright might be able to "... suggest an architect who is capable of carrying on the ideas and ideals you have established," might he have been aware that Wright undoubtedly believed there was no one who fit that description? The letter goes on to describe a building site in a beautiful, country setting with plenty of land and space to work with. A particularly good touch is the introduction of skepticism on the part of "... local builders about the possibility of working into our house native lumber from our trees and stone from our quarry." Wright must have loved the idea that he might, once again, have an opportunity to fly in the face of tradition. Then Dad introduces a young family which has outgrown its present home and needs a new one, but has a limited budget with which to accomplish this. He doesn't hesitate to spell out the limits of that budget by forthrightly stating the amount he has in mind. He finishes by handing Wright a challenge that has been carefully wrapped in another compliment to his skills.

A week later Dad received a reply from Eugene Masselink, Wright's Secretary, saying that he would forward Dad's letter to Wright, who was in New York for a few days before going on to Arizona. He said, "I feel sure that he would like to design your house for you and I am enclosing a sheet describing Mr. Wright's architectural services." [1]

A month later, in a letter dated January 23, 1946, Dad received his first letter from Frank Lloyd Wright:

"Dear Mr. Grant: Of course it is practical. Why don't you drive up to Taliesin Mid-West, Spring Green, Wisconsin early next May." [2]

Mother and Dad were ecstatic; possibly also somewhat awed by the turn of events. What had they started? It was almost too much to comprehend, but the goal they had set for themselves was now in sight. This was the beginning. The end would be a long way off, but it began to seem a bit closer. Now it was time to get busy. There was so much to be done, so much planning to do, and there would be a lot of hard work ahead. But the clock had started to tick and they were ready to go!

The reference to local builders in Dad's letter was well grounded in fact. Once Mother and Dad had decided they would build a house, they discovered they had lots of questions that needed answers. One of the biggest question-marks was the suitability of the stone for building purposes. Although they thought the stone was beautiful, there had definitely been indications from some that it might not work as a building material. This was certainly something they needed to know as soon as possible, so Dad contacted as many of the area's stonemasons as he could find, and asked them to give us their opinions.

People in eastern Iowa have been building things out of limestone for many years. There is an abundance of good stone all over the area. During the time he was quarrying our stone, Dad became a self-taught geology student. At night he read about how the stone came to be in the ground and, during the day, he dug it out. As children, we became intimately acquainted with the stone and learned lessons in geology we might normally have avoided. With all that stone around, finding people willing to give their opinion wasn't difficult. The most common source of limestone in the area was near Anamosa, a town about 20 miles northeast of Cedar Rapids, noted primarily as both the location for abundant stone quarries and the state reformatory. Dad talked to builders and stone contractors for names of good stonemasons. Stonemasons take a great deal of pride in their work. They consider themselves to be several cuts above mere bricklayers, because they feel that laying stone requires artistic judgment that cannot be learned by just anyone.

In the meantime, Dad and Mother had managed to harvest a sizeable pile of stone by prying it out of the exposed face of the quarry. But as the masons came, one-by-one, to give their opinion of the stone it became distressingly obvious that they didn't think much of it. Most were polite, wanting to please, yet all felt the stone was too difficult to work with. Some even ventured the opinion that it would crumble away with a few year's exposure to the elements. Building with stone, at that time, meant that you took thick slabs of stone and broke off the sides with a stone chisel and hammer to make uniform blocks. Those blocks were then plastered with mortar and stuck into place to raise the walls (much like laying brick). Our stone, however, was of varying thickness, was unusually hard and didn't break easily into straight edges. But the final straw was contributed by the mason who came one afternoon with a full quota of self-confidence and a full wad of chewing tobacco. He eyed the pile of rock for several minutes, kicking the stones around for a better look, and finally said, "There ain't a stone worth using in that whole pile if you ask me."

As he delivered his opinion, he also delivered himself of a huge stream of tobacco juice which landed right in the middle of the pile. Since they had, in fact, asked him, there wasn't much they could do except to thank him for his time and opinion. I feel sure it was necessary to restrain Mother from saying a great deal more than that. Since she had driven quite a distance to pick him up and would have to drive him home again, she felt his opinion was unnecessarily candid.

Morale was low at the Grant household as one mason after another offered the same judgment. Oh, there was plenty of good building stone at Anamosa or at Stone City, nearby. But if Mother and Dad had to buy stone, the house would become impossibly expensive and it would be years before they could afford to build it. It was vital to the whole plan that they use the stone from our quarry. And we thought the stone was beautiful.

A family friend, Ron Henderson, had been convinced from the

beginning that the stone was good for building. Dad valued his opinion because he knew it came from a man who was not only a skilled contractor but an ardent lover of nature, with a deep appreciation for all it had to offer. Ron played a large part in the story of the Grant house, and he had become a friend in a somewhat unusual way.

In 1944, work started on the excavation for a house that was to be built across the street from us. As Mother worked in her garden, she became fascinated with the intricacies involved in excavating with a bulldozer. Soon she dropped all pretence of being out in the garden for any other reason and just stood and watched. Since she assumed that the machine's operator was too involved in his task to have noticed her, she was totally unprepared when, a day or two into the project, he stopped his machine, climbed down and walked up to her.

"Okay," he said to her, "now you try it."

"What?" she could barely stammer out.

"You get up there and operate the machine for a while. I know you can do it because you've been standing there watching me all this time."

Mother didn't have to be asked twice. That was the beginning of a friendship with Ron Henderson we enjoyed until his tragic accidental death in 1950.

Dad decided to rely on Ron's judgment about the stone and proceed on the assumption that Wright would reach the same conclusion. As if to emphasize that decision, a piece of good news came from another, unexpected, source. During a casual conversation with Roy Choate, Dad learned that the building foundations for LaPlant-Choate, the road equipment company founded by Choate's father some 20 years earlier, were made of stone from the same source we were now quarrying. Choate said the foundations were as strong now as the day they were built.

At the time all this controversy about the stone was taking place, the native timber idea was not being met with much enthusiasm, either. One of our neighbors, who ran a family-owned lumber business, was of the opinion that it would cost more in the long-run to harvest and process our own trees than it would to buy the lumber from a local lumber yard. Dad and Mother were willing to do many things, but sawing up logs into boards was not going to be one of them. Fortunately, they had the wisdom to know just where it was necessary to draw the line. The native timber still stands.

On May 3, 1946, Dad wrote again to Wright, reminding him that he had suggested they visit him in the spring to talk over plans for a new home. If the invitation was still good, they would like to come during the next two or three weeks, at a time that was convenient for him.

Wright's reply came the following week: "Dear Douglas Grant: Come up last weekend in May?" [3]

FOUR

I Believe You Are Sincere

Mother and Dad drove to Spring Green, Wisconsin the last weekend in May 1946 to meet Frank Lloyd Wright for the first time. They had seen many photographs of Taliesin, but they were not adequately prepared for the dramatic impact of that remarkable house. Access to Taliesin is accomplished by a long, winding drive that permits only occasional tantalizing glimpses of the house through the trees; anyone approaching for the first time cannot help but feel a mounting sense of excitement. As the last bend is rounded, the house comes fully into view; not an ostentatious mansion that dominates its surroundings and towers high above the viewer, but a deceptively simple, yet majestic, expression of one man's belief that his dwelling should be an integral part of the place where he has chosen to build it. This house hugs the hilltop, spreading out in several directions, and its low flat shape, emphasized by the broad overhanging eaves, long balconies and wide chimneys, strongly resembles the great natural outcroppings of stone that project from many of the surrounding hillsides. It is logical and appropriate that the house Frank Lloyd Wright built for himself should look like this.

Mother and Dad spent very little time alone with Wright on that first trip; they talked with him for only an hour. The interview was evidently intended as an opportunity for him to become acquainted with them, learn something about their lives, and to evaluate their motives for wanting him to design their house. The discussion was mostly a philosophical one, with Wright developing a number of abstract architectural concepts. He was genuinely interested, though, to hear they had built their first house themselves, and he admired their determination to do so a second time. The idea of Mother and Dad quarrying and using their own stone appealed greatly to Wright and, although he had not yet seen any of the stone, he waved aside any suggestions that it might not be suitable for building as nonsense uttered by those who were too set in their ways to appreciate a bonanza when they saw one. There was some discussion of finances; Mother and Dad felt it was important that he understand that their resources were limited. He did acknowledge their situation, but Wright was not overly fond of talking about what things cost and the topic was dispensed with early in the conversation.

Most of the two day visit was devoted to the various Taliesin rituals that traditionally occupied each weekend. On Saturday evening, dinner was held at the theater, prepared as usual by the apprentices and served by them on small individual tables facing the stage. After dinner, Wright spoke to the assembled Fellowship, family and several guests, including Mother and Dad; his talk was followed by a slide presentation of Fellowship projects currently in progress. Mrs. Wright was a gracious hostess and seemed genuinely concerned with her guests' comfort as she said goodnight and made certain everyone knew what time breakfast would be served in the morning. The next day, Mother and Dad were given a comprehensive tour of Taliesin by one or another of the young members of the Fellowship, who Wright called "the boys". They also had ample time in which to walk about the grounds alone, wondering what kind of impression they had made on Wright. He had told them, during their discussion the previous day, that he did not design houses for everyone who asked him.

"You must want one of my houses because you love it, not because you want to impress your friends and neighbors," he told them.

Each Sunday evening, Mr. and Mrs. Wright, the Fellowship and invited guests gathered in the great Taliesin living room for dinner and an evening of music, theater or dance performed by the students, most of whom were talented in several areas. Everyone attended the affair dressed in formal attire, a touch that contributed a degree of magnificence to the occasion that might otherwise have been difficult to achieve, considering that most of these people saw each other every day. Mother and Dad, new to the routine, had not thought to bring formal clothes. Mother thought seriously about appearing at dinner wearing the beautiful, hand-loomed spread that covered the bed in their guest room, but she was deterred by the thought that Mrs. Wright would almost certainly recognize it and might not construe the gesture as a complimentary one. They resigned themselves to attending the gala affair in street clothes, feeling uncomfortably drab.

Only at the end of the evening, as they thanked their host and hostess and said goodbye before the drive back to Cedar Rapids, did Wright give them his decision. With great solemnity, he drew them aside, saying,

"I like you. You are honest people and I believe you are sincere in your reasons for wanting one of my houses. I will design your home for you."

He advised them to send him as much information about the building site as they could: topographical drawings, photographs, anything that would help him to form an idea of the setting for this house. Next, he asked them to draw up a detailed list of requirements, ideas and features they wanted incorporated into the design. When that was done, they must come back to Taliesin for another visit, at which time they would all sit down together and plan the house. And, finally, they must bring the children next time; it was important to Wright that he meet everyone in the Grant family.

Dad wrote to Wright again in August 1946. He had been having difficulty finding a surveyor who had the time or the inclination to make a contour drawing of the site. Finally, however, he had located the right man for the job, the drawings were in process, and the finished product would be sent off to Taliesin as soon as it was ready. In the meantime, Mother and Dad wanted to schedule another visit to discuss the project, and they communicated that fact to Wright. Within a few days, Wright replied that they would be welcome at Taliesin as soon as they had gathered together everything they would need for the meeting.

When the surveyor had finished his work and the topographic drawings were ready, Dad sent them to Wright, along with photographs taken from various points at the site and from every conceivable angle—all marked carefully to indicate the compass direction.

At the time all of this was taking place, the Country was in the aftermath of World War II. There had never been any question of Dad being required to fight in the war. His job as news broadcaster and radio station Program Manager qualified him as "Essential to the War Effort". As children we were not much aware of the war. When I learned many years later that my husband's family, in New Jersey, had been required to blacken the top half of their automobile headlights and provide their home with black-out curtains, I realized that we were much more sheltered from the war and its ramifications out there in the Midwest. Of course we knew what was going on; our dad described it on the news twice a day. He had become a small celebrity in town as a result of those broadcasts on WMT Radio. There wasn't much of a newspaper in Cedar Rapids, so people got the war news by listening to the radio. Dad always prided himself on learning to pronounce all of the Japanese, French and Italian names correctly, and any German names were given the full treatment—umlauts and all!

While the war was going on, it was difficult to get many things that we had always taken for granted: gasoline and automobile tires, meat, butter, sugar, leather shoes and nylon stockings and cigarettes (the latter not a hardship, since no one in the family smoked). Anything that needed to be imported from somewhere else was almost impossible to get. We particularly missed the bananas for our morning cereal. Everything went to "the war effort". Things were either rationed or we did without them.

Since we had a lot of land, Dad was convinced that we should begin raising a great deal of our own food. Because he grew up in cities, he had always harbored a secret desire to Live off the Land, and he was deep into the writings of Louis Bromfield at the time. Mother, who had grown up on farms, was somewhat less enthusiastic, having lived off the land more than she ever wanted to again, but she agreed it would make a lot of sense. Dad began reading everything he could find on running a small farm. There was a steady stream of County Extension Bulletins and U.S. Department of Agriculture publications arriving in the mail on a regular basis. Fortunately, Mother had a great deal of practical experience to add to the project, and they plunged in with a vengeance. We had an enormous vegetable garden, with every vegetable you could think of and some you wouldn't. We started a fruit orchard; we already had wild blackberries and gooseberries. We also had chickens, two little piglets, five geese, a steer for beef and a beautiful gentle brown cow, named Honeysuckle, for milk, cream and butter.

How did Mother and Dad do it? At the time I was oblivious to the amount of time and effort that was involved. Dad worked at the radio station from nine to five, then went back for the ten o'clock news broadcast. David and I were obliged to do some weeding in the garden and feed the weeds to the chickens, but those were not tasks we entered into with any degree of enthusiasm or consistency. I know the answer now; Dad did a lot of it, but Mother did most of it. She hoed and weeded, fed the chickens and gathered the eggs, separated the cream from the milk, churned the butter, helped harvest the garden and preserved the food for use during the winter months. Oh, yes, she was also raising three children, cooking, cleaning and making most of our clothes. She didn't have to milk the cow, though. Dad hired Mrs. Rudish, from the Czech family in the valley, to milk our cow twice a day for a small cash payment.

The only thing we couldn't grow was sugar, but nature provided there, as well. Dad discovered a tree on the property that bees had been filling full of honey for several years. Bees, however, do not let you just come in and help yourself, so a neighbor volunteered to help Dad get the honey out in exchange for a portion of it. After discussions with people who had done this before, they tackled the job, wearing protective netting. They cut down the old, hollow tree and mesmerized the bees with smoky torches while they harvested wash tubs full of honey. That solved the problem of a sugar shortage for a long time.

This small-scale farming operation, and the space it required, was one of the many considerations Mother and Dad needed to address as they prepared to draw up a list of what they wanted to include in the design for their new house. It wasn't going to be easy, however. They had no difficulty coming up with everything they wanted, but they had a budget to consider and they knew they would have to keep their enthusiasm within certain boundaries. Still, it must have been exciting for them to believe they would have some control over what would be included in this house, and that they would soon be sitting down to talk it over with Frank Lloyd Wright.

FIVE

I Have It All Right Here

As we set out upon our journey to Spring Green that morning in 1946, I had no idea what to expect. Mother and Dad had told us in great detail about their first visit to Wright's home in Wisconsin and it sounded much more exotic than anything I had experienced to date. The three youngest members of the Grant family had only recently learned who Frank Lloyd Wright was. We had been told by Mother and Dad that he was a famous architect, and we looked at pictures of buildings he had designed in the well-worn copy of *Architectural Forum* magazine that had been leafed through many times by now. David and I, and our four year-old sister, Linda, were not entirely clear as to exactly what it was an architect did, but we understood perfectly well that he had recently become an important part of our parents' world.

It was decided that Linda was too young to make the trip this time. Occasional demonstrations of sibling rivalry were not uncommon in our household, and there was no question that a ratio of one adult per child worked best when a situation required domestic tranquility—which this one clearly did. Frank Lloyd Wright could meet Linda another time.

We set out before dawn that morning, somewhat apprehensive, but excited about what we were going to find at the end of our trip. Mother and Dad had succeeded in making us understand that this was an extremely important visit; today we would talk to Mr. Wright about the kind of house we would build some day.

The drive from Cedar Rapids to Spring Green, Wisconsin, a distance of about 140 miles, was a memorable one. Dad always liked to get an early start to avoid as much traffic as possible and, although the distance wasn't far, automobile trips took longer in those days. There were no four-lane highways in that part of the country, and if you got stuck behind a big truck you could be there for a long time. Mother and Dad had carefully saved gas rationing stamps in preparation for this trip, but there wasn't much they could do about tires. We had at least two blowouts on the way up, due to the poor quality of the wartime patched tires we were still obliged to use. At one point, we pulled into a service station (service stations actually had a staff to help their customers!) only to have the attendants take one look at us and back off to stare from a distance. When Dad got out to question this strange behavior, his attention was directed to the left rear tire which had a bubble on the sidewall the size of a large grapefruit. Fortunately, the tortured rubber held together until someone let out the pressure and the tire could be patched and put back into service.

We reached Spring Green shortly after noon and, as everyone was very hungry and a little cranky, Dad found a small restaurant where we could get out, stretch our legs and have some lunch, thereby ensuring a more peaceful arrival at Taliesin. As David and I were preparing to get out of the car, however, Mother suddenly said something quite surprising. She made sure she had our attention and then she said, "If anyone asks you where you are going today, don't tell them we are going to visit Mr. Wright."

We looked at her with amazement, but her solemn tone told us not to question this pronouncement. She needn't have worried; no one in town asked and we certainly didn't volunteer the information. Our brief visit to Spring Green went by without incident and the subject never came up again. It wasn't until many years later that I guessed at what must have been behind Mother's uncharacteristic behavior. Frank Lloyd Wright had taken a vigorous and outspoken anti-war stance during World War II which couldn't have endeared him to the local citizenry, since I'm sure many of the townspeople had sons, husbands and fathers who fought in the war. Such thoughts were considered to be highly unpatriotic at the time. In addition, Wright's iconoclastic lifestyle at Taliesin over the years, coupled with his nonchalance regarding financial obligations, undoubtedly produced ill-feeling on the part of some who lived in Spring Green, so it is quite likely that there were many in town who did not regard Wright with the same respect with which my family did. But it seems remarkable to me that Mother found it necessary to sound a note of caution that day; she certainly had no intention of explaining the reason to David and me. I wish I had thought to ask my parents in later years if they had been much disturbed by Wright's political beliefs or his colorful reputation, and if such things affected the regard they had for him. My guess is that it made no difference at all, at least to my father. Mother was a bit more sensitive to public opinion than Dad was, and it surfaced that day as she voiced her concern about our visit. It was a small thing, which David and I put out of our minds as soon as we tucked into our lunch, but I never entirely forgot it.

The details of my first visit to Taliesin have faded in the intervening years, but the visual and emotional impression that it made on me has never diminished. I was dramatically affected by the beauty of the place and the remarkable atmosphere created by those unfamiliar surroundings. I had never seen anything like this in all of my eleven years! Mother and Dad had told us many times about their first visit, and we had looked at photographs of Taliesin until we knew them by heart, but we really had no idea of what to expect once we arrived there. I was terribly impressed, for instance, by the automobiles parked in the courtyard when we arrived—many of them foreign models—all painted Wright's favorite Cherokee Red. David liked the peacocks that strutted about the grounds, although we never succeeded in getting them to display their spectacular tail feathers. When Mrs. Wright learned that we greatly admired the peacocks, she graciously offered to give Mother some peacock eggs to take home with us so we could raise our own. I'm not sure Mrs. Wright fully understood the fundamentals involved in turning eggs into peacocks but, in any case, it was a generous gesture on her part. Anyway, after she heard the loud, high-pitched screams the peacocks made, Mother decided not to remind Mrs. Wright of her offer.

I believe young children are often the keenest observers of their environment. They have not yet learned what adults consider "important" and are, therefore, free to form their own opinions of what they see. Because children were usually called upon to be "seen but not heard" in those days, they weren't required to engage in the amenities that occupy adults on social occasions and, consequently, were able to evaluate situations and people pretty accurately. I suspect there was never any danger of misbehavior that day. David and I noticed the extraordinary respect and deference with which everyone, including our parents, treated Mr. Wright; yet, at the same time, we felt welcome and important at Taliesin. Young as we were, we knew it was a privilege to be there.

It was a chilly autumn day and a fire crackled cheerfully in the big stone fireplace in Wright's study. There were wooly sheepskins and colorful pillows thrown over the benches and built-in couches, and there were colorful rugs on the floor. Displayed in vases at nearly every corner and ledge were enormous cut branches of brilliantly colored fall foliage, which presented a vivid contrast to the neutral tones of the stone and wood of which the house was constructed. There were books, papers and drawing materials scattered about the tables, but here and there among these implements of work were such delightful surprises as squat little bronze Buddhas, burnished metal trays and delicate Japanese prints of enchanting scenes. The effect created by this wonderfully hospitable room was perfectly suited to the stately old, white-haired gentleman who presided over it. I had never before seen anyone quite like Mr. Wright and, dressed as he was in a suit of soft material, old-fashioned collar and string tie, with his famous cape thrown loosely around his shoulders, he made a profound impression on me. I fell in love with Taliesin the first time I saw it; I had been there for only a short time when I decided that this was the way to live! Taliesin was my idea of gracious living and, if Mother and Dad could somehow manage to get us a house like this one, I was all for it. I don't remember what David did or said, and neither does he, but there is one thing about that visit I remember very well. Before we were sent out to a courtyard to amuse ourselves while the adults held their discussion, Mr. Wright called me over and gathered me onto his lap. He asked me what I would like to have in our new house, and to my parents' complete surprise, since they were hearing this for the first time, I replied with no hesitation at all, "I want a fireplace in my room."

Later, when we had our first look at the preliminary drawings, there it was—a fireplace in Donna's bedroom! Mother and Dad were surprised and amused when they discovered it, but I'd never had any doubt at all that Mr. Wright would do as I had asked.

At Wright's request, Mother and Dad had spent a great deal of time putting together a list of the things they wanted him to include in our house. This list, along with a general consideration of the family's requirements and expectations, was to be the main topic of discussion at this conference. Wright had left his reading glasses in another room so, when the list was produced, he asked Dad to read it aloud. The list, typed on yellow copy paper from the radio station newsroom, noted various features that should be considered for each room or area and described the various family activities that would take place in those spaces. For instance:

Living Room: We needed a large room we could use for family activities and for social gatherings. Mother and Dad enjoyed entertaining, and their idea of a good evening was having their friends gathered around for cocktails, a good dinner and lots of stimulating conversation. Our present living room was tiny, with limited seating and, since we children slept in the rooms above, we might as well have been down there with the guests because we heard everything that was said. Dad was really describing what we had already, but on a grander scale. We wanted a big fireplace, lots of bookshelves for our continually growing collection, a built-in phonograph/radio with space for record storage (this was back in the days of 78 rpm records). Possibly influenced by the living room at Taliesin, Dad requested space for a grand piano. We had an old upright piano which Dad played occasionally, and on which I was supposed to practice my piano lessons, but somehow it lacked the romance of a big concert grand. We asked for a dining area close to the living room but, since dinner parties at the Grant house were small and informal, there would be no need for a large formal dining room. Finally, we wanted the living room to open onto a terrace area so that we could move our dining and entertaining outside when weather permitted.

Kitchen: It needed to be convenient to the dining area. Mother did all her own cooking as well as serving and clearing, but this was long before the days of the open kitchen/dining room and kitchens were often stuck back into a remote part of the house as if to deny that food was prepared somewhere before it reached the table. Mother spent a lot of time in the kitchen, and she wanted it to be full of light with a good view of the outdoors, with windows that opened for ventilation.

Master Bedroom: Mother and Dad badly needed a space of their own, as far as possible from the living room and the children's rooms. Although we were still young, they knew the day would come when we began to do our own entertaining and they wanted to have a good, quiet retreat when necessary. A separate bath area was mandatory. At present, five family members shared one bathroom (a tiny one at that) and the logistics were exceedingly complicated, to say the least. Dad wanted a space for a desk and bookshelves, and Mother needed an area where she could do her sewing. Finally, if it wasn't too much to ask, they very much wanted a fireplace in their bedroom.

In General: A great deal of everyone's spare time took place outdoors—Mother's gardening, Dad's building and maintenance chores and harvesting of firewood, and the children's outdoor play in all seasons. For that reason, we needed a locker-room sort of place, with an outside entrance where work and play clothes could be stored—boots and snowsuits in winter, play equipment in summer—and with a shower and toilet.

At the time this list was compiled, Mother and Dad were still running their small-scale farming operation with cows, chickens, etc. Dad asked for space in the house to keep the cream separator and other dairy equipment, and he requested storage space for all the products of Mother's copious canning and preserving efforts. It didn't occur to them that, once they began the construction process, their farm work would dwindle to the barest minimum. They would have time for nothing except building the house. Finally, Dad asked for a workshop with tool storage and a small area for his photography, complete with darkroom.

At the conclusion of the discussion that day, Wright smiled, paused dramatically and then said,

"I have already designed your house."

Still considerably awed by this remarkable man, Mother and Dad could only glance at each other uneasily and respond with a confused,

"You have?"

"Oh, yes," he replied. And, pointing to his forehead, he said, "It's all right here. All I have to do now is put it on paper."

A House for Mr. and Mrs. Douglas Grant

"Dear Mr. Grant: We are sending you today the preliminary studies for your house.

"Mr. Wright asked me to mail you the enclosed statement (for $600). With best wishes to Mrs. Grant and the family!"

Sincerely yours,

Eugene Masselink, Secretary to Frank Lloyd Wright

November 19, 1946 [4]

The preliminary drawings were beautiful! They were drawn in full color and showed perspectives of all four sides, as well as the floor plans for two levels. The house was so elegant that it was hard to believe it was meant for us. But there it was: "A House for Mr. and Mrs. Douglas Grant: Frank Lloyd Wright, Architect". The perspective of the house from the south was particularly stunning. It began with a long row of rooms that seemed to emerge right out of the hill and culminated, high above the surrounding countryside, in a majestic two-story living room, surrounded on three sides by a "curtain" of glass. It was exciting for Mother

South Perspective. Copyright Frank Lloyd Wright Foundation

FOR MR AND MRS DOUGLAS GRANT
LLOYD WRIGHT ARCHITECT

and Dad to see the drawings for the first time, to compare them with their list of requirements for the house, and to look for what had been included and what had not. Miraculously, almost everything they asked for was there; there were a few things they were not entirely comfortable with, that Dad would convey to Wright, but they were not major problems and could probably be solved as the plans progressed. We had good reason to be excited about these drawings. Not only were they beautiful to look at, but they were our first glimpse of what would prove to be one of the finest examples of Wright's Usonian houses.

The term "Usonian" was one used by Frank Lloyd Wright to replace "American" when describing the unique style of architecture he began in 1936 with the Herbert Jacobs house. Usonian houses were usually one-story, with no basement, attic or garage. They were comparatively small in square footage, but they provided a feeling of light and space, since nearly every room had access to the outside. Much of the furniture was built in, as were most of the lighting fixtures. Heating was provided by Wright's concept of Gravity Heating, which consisted of hot water pumped through pipes embedded in the concrete or stone floors. The simplicity of their design was intended to make them affordable by middle-income families. Although they did not know it before they met Frank Lloyd Wright, my parents were the perfect candidates for a Usonian house.

The preliminary drawings of the Grant house show it to be a long rectangle, measuring a little over three thousand square feet; the design is based on four-foot square modules, as are many of Wright's Usonian houses. Somewhat uncharacteristic of a Usonian, the house is on two levels, with a two-story living room at one end. The roof is a great slab of reinforced concrete 127 feet long, turned up at the edges and cantilevered to provide a sheltering overhang on each side, as much as eight feet at one end. The walls are of stone. One enters on the upper level, from the east, on a grade with the driveway and the carport. Entry is into a loggia,

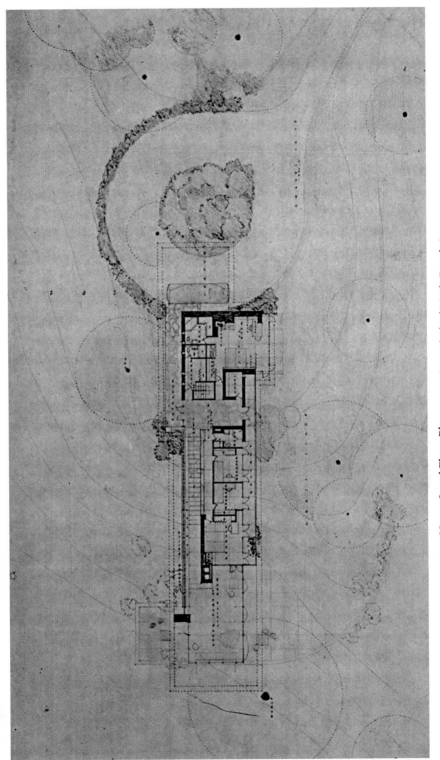

Upper Level Floor Plan. Copyright Frank Lloyd Wright Foundation

or entrance hall, with a long corridor to the right that provides access to the three children's bedrooms and bath. To the left, directly upon entry, is the locker/mud room and access to a utility stairway to the lower level. Beyond the entrance to the locker room, also to the left is the hallway to the master bed/sitting room. Directly opposite the main entrance, is a door that leads to a covered balcony that runs the entire length of the children's bedrooms, to which each room has access. The last in the line of children's rooms overlooks the two-story living room by means of a casement window. Directly to the right of the main entrance is a long stairway, which descends between two stone walls and emerges into the living room below.

The living room is in direct contrast to the rest of the house. The roof is supported by massive stone piers and has walls of glass doors and windows on three sides. The view is to the west, north and south; there are terraces on both north and south sides, which are accessed from the living room. There is a very large stone fireplace, nearly six feet tall, at the northeast corner of the room. Three low steps lead up to the dining area, which also has a fireplace; beyond that is the kitchen. On the other side of the kitchen, the lower level is underground. That space is devoted to utility, storage and laundry areas. The drawings indicated that the entrance walkway, the grand stairway and the floors in the loggia were to be of flagstone; the rest of the floors appeared to be concrete.

I have deliberately limited this description of the house to the way it appeared to us in the drawings; at this point, this was all we really knew about the house. By the time the working drawings were completed, several things had changed as a result of Dad's discussions with Wright: notably, the floors of the living room and its two adjoining terraces were changed from concrete to flagstone and an exit to the outdoors was added from the utility area.

Some of those changes were suggested in Dad's letter to Gene Masselink on November 28, 1946:

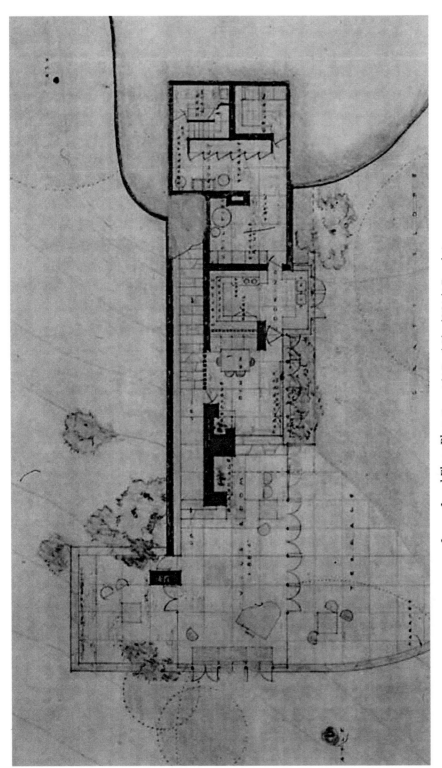

Lower Level Floor Plan. Copyright Frank Lloyd Wright Foundation

"... The preliminary studies of our house arrived in good order and they are wonderful; better, even than we dared hope! The only additional suggestions we have are minor ones, and we have a few questions.

"First, the suggestions: Mrs. Grant would like to have a more direct outside entrance to the kitchen-utility-laundry area. She feels that the back stair-way is a round-about means of gaining access to the laundry room, particularly if one is carrying a heavy load of laundry. Also, there are frequent errands in and out of the kitchen which would make a more direct outside entrance desirable. Frankly, we have no idea how this can be accomplished, and if it means substantially redesigning the house we would prefer to waive the idea entirely. However, we thought Mr. Wright might be able to accomplish the purpose without extensive changes.

"... Now for the questions. Do you have copies of the drawings we received or shall we return them? If they should be returned, should we send them to Spring Green or to Arizona?

"We are unable to determine from the drawings what types of partitions are intended between the dining area and the kitchen and between the dining area and the hallway.

"We note the floors in the loggia and the steps are of stone. Are the other floors concrete?

"What types of partitions are planned between the bedrooms? I assume the bearing partitions are of stone.

"Shouldn't the well for our water supply be located in relation to the house? How about placing the well and pump in a pit adjacent to the utility room with access for servicing the pump through a small door directly from the utility room?

"Let me emphasize how pleased we are, generally, with the preliminary plans. We can hardly wait to get started. Our check for $600 is enclosed (representing 3% of the proposed building cost, as per the contract with the architect)."

The letter was duly acknowledged and forwarded to Wright who was in Arizona. On December 10, 1946, he replied:

"My dear Douglas Grant: You have the originals and may keep them until working plans could do you some good.

"Sound proof and fireproof partitions between dining room, kitchen and corridor—with movable screen at openings.

"Other floors are concrete.

"Bearing partitions—insulated block walls.

"Regarding your suggestion for well, etc.: All right.

Faithfully,

Frank Lloyd Wright" [5]

In March of 1947, Wright requested that the drawings be returned so work could begin on the working drawings. Somewhat regretfully, Dad packaged up the drawings and sent them off to Taliesin West. In an air mail letter to Wright (undated), Dad noted:

"Dear Mr. Wright: At the request of Gene Masselink I have sent the plans for our house. We are delighted to know that you are now ready to begin the working drawings. Our much-anticipated house seems that much nearer realization ..."

The arrival of the drawings was acknowledged on March 31, 1947, by Gene Masselink, who added, "... Mr. Wright is at work on the finished drawings." [6]

It was difficult to give up those drawings; they made the concept of our house real, and we all spent a lot of time looking at them and trying to imagine what it would be like to live there. I remember pouring over every detail whenever I got the chance. On the one hand, it was exciting to think we would someday live in this magical house but, at the same time, part of me was saying, "We'll never really do it; we'll never live in a place like this."

I should have known my parents a little better than that.

SEVEN

You Get the Stone Out

During the period following the end of World War II, the drafting room at Taliesin started to take on a new vibrancy, as hundreds of requests for Wright's services began to arrive from all over the world. Several more apprentices were added to the Fellowship, and Wright was eager to take on the new work as he approached his 80th birthday. From 1943 to 1946 he conceived and developed plans for the Guggenheim Museum in New York, a commission he had worked hard to get. In 1947, Wright turned what had originally been a relatively simple request by Edgar J. Kaufmann for a parking garage in Pittsburgh into a grand design for a garage and a civic center on the same site. At the same time, he was working on designs for many small residences; it must have delighted him that suddenly everyone wanted a Frank Lloyd Wright design. By 1948 the Johnson Wax Building was well under way, the Lowell Walter house in Quasqueton, Iowa was under construction, the second house for Mr. and Mrs. Herbert Jacobs had entered the building stage and Wright had started designs for the Unitarian Church in Madison, Wisconsin.

It's probably not surprising, then, that Dad hadn't heard anything from Taliesin since the end of March 1947. He wrote to Wright in July of that year:

"How are things progressing on the working drawings for our house? Should we begin to think about accumulating stone or other building materials on our site?"

Wright replied that the drawings would be finished soon and asked for a sample of the stone from our quarry. Although there had been some discussion with Wright about the limestone in the Grant quarry, he had not yet seen any of it. He gave no credibility to the negative opinions rendered by nearly everyone Dad had consulted and appeared to accept Dad's view that the stone might be suitable for building. So, with considerable trepidation, Dad crated up some of the stone, taking care to select the most representative pieces. He arranged with a local trucking company to send the crate to Taliesin in Wisconsin—enduring the inevitable jokes such as, "What have you got in here, rocks?"

His August 13th letter explained:

"I have shipped to you samples of stone from the abandoned quarry on our property near the site of our new home. There appear to be two kinds of stone there. One type is the gray limestone in strata which vary in thickness from one-fourth of an inch to about three or four inches. The other type is a brown limestone which lies in strata varying from about two inches to nearly 16 inches thick. I included samples of all but the thickest brown stone which was too heavy to ship easily.

"If any of this stone is satisfactory I think it could be removed quite inexpensively. The overlay of topsoil varies from two feet to about four or five feet. Then comes the gray limestone in various strata totaling about four feet. Below this is the brown stone."

Wright's reply, nearly three weeks later, consisted of one sentence:

The limestone quarry today.

"Dear Douglas Grant: Why not mix the two types?" [7]

The letter was greeted by Mother and Dad with enthusiasm and relief, for they interpreted it to mean that Wright approved of the stone. The house that had seemed at times to be only an unreachable ideal, immediately began to take on a form that could be imagined, now that they knew it would be made of the stone from our quarry. If Wright had decided the stone was unacceptable, I don't know what they would have done. Buying stone from another source was out of the question for them, and they couldn't imagine a house made of any other material. It's entirely possible, of course, that Wright remembered what Dad had told him earlier about the judgments passed on the stone's suitability by the local "experts". Never one to accept such facts at face value, I expect he very much enjoyed proving the experts wrong.

Now, of course, it was necessary to think of ways to get it out of the ground in large quantities and haul it up to the building site. In mid September, Dad wrote again to Wright and asked if he should begin making arrangements for having the stone quarried. Was there someone in the area that Wright could suggest for the job? Probably the reason Dad thought Wright might have someone in mind is that he had recently designed a house of stone for Dr. and Mrs. Alvin Miller, in Charles City, Iowa. Presumably, he would have been familiar with the methods the Millers employed to obtain their stone. Mother and Dad must have discussed the possibility that they could quarry the stone themselves, and surely they would have mentioned it to Wright during one of the early visits to Taliesin. But they may have thought he wouldn't approve of two amateurs taking on a job that was so vitally important to the whole building project. Therefore, the answer, brief and to the point, must have come as a shock, but also as a great relief, "Dear Grant: You get the stone out and cord it up for hauling."[8]

Mother and Dad had acquired many practical skills by this time, but quarrying stone was not one of them. They had, of course, already assembled quite a pile of stone on the site in anticipation of the time they could begin building, and to convince themselves that they were doing something useful while they waited for Wright to finish the drawings. Dad pried the stone loose with a crowbar, then he and Mother loaded it into our little green two-wheeled trailer and hauled the load up to the site with the army-surplus Jeep we used for a work vehicle. But there is more to quarrying stone than loading and hauling, and Dad eventually reached the point where he had removed every stone that he could. It was time to blast more of it loose. They would have to learn to use explosives before they could go any further, and that was definitely not a thing you wanted to learn by trial and error.

Their friend and advisor on construction matters, the aforementioned Ron Henderson, advised against the use of dynamite; the stone was brittle and dynamite would shatter it. Instead, he felt that black powder was better for their purposes. It was relatively easy to use and the charge could be controlled so that only a big shudder was produced, not a tremendous boom. The stone would be loosened gently and broken up only enough so that it would come out of the ground easily. He thought he'd heard that the state prison at Anamosa had some black powder that might be for sale. As it happened, an old high school classmate of Mother's was the Warden at the prison. When she called him, he told her they did have a supply left over from the days when they had quarried stone there and they would gladly sell it. Mother and Dad drove up one afternoon, bought several 25 pound tins of it, loaded them carefully into the trunk of the car and drove home. David got to go with them and, although only seven years old, he remembers the awe he felt as they approached their destination, knowing perfectly well what prisons were used for. He was not allowed out of the car, but Mother's friend, the Warden, had some fun teasing him. David had a very short crew-cut at the time, so the Warden said to him, "Wouldn't you like to stay with us for a while, son? You've already got the right haircut for this place!"

Even though Dad had done some reading on the subject, and he was told that black powder doesn't explode on impact and, in the form they were buying, is less likely to ignite when lit with a match or spark, it still must have been a nervous drive home. Since Linda and I had not been invited to go along, there had been plenty of time for us to speculate on the awesome possibilities of the situation and to pass them along to anyone who would listen. As a result, there was a sizeable group of spectators on hand when the trunk-load of black powder arrived; all of the neighborhood kids had mysteriously learned of the event and had mustered for the occasion. Everyone watched in respectful silence as the explosives were unloaded gently and stored in the former pig house, which had been fitted with a lock for the purpose. The entire Grant family had, of course, gained instant prestige. The main topic of conversation at neighborhood dinner tables that night is easy to guess.

Mother and Dad quarried stone all that fall and as long into the following winter as weather and temperature would allow. Working with black powder turned out to be reasonably simple. When it first became obvious that they would be quarrying the stone themselves, Dad had hired Ron Henderson to excavate the soil, or overburden, from the top of the rock. Now, all they had to do was decide where they wanted to drill holes for the explosive and then do it. The following year, Dad hired a neighbor's son, home from college for the summer, to drill the holes. They had a heavy-duty drill with an old crank-start air compressor to power it and they drilled holes down through the stone to a depth of 12 feet. Occasionally the drill would get stuck in the rock far below. They were usually able to get it back out; but, if you visit the quarry site today, there is a place where the top portion of a drill bit is still sticking out of the ground—testament to the fact that not everything went as smoothly as it could have.

When the time came to use the black powder, Ron found Dad a specialist for the job, known in the trade as a "Powder Monkey". After a hole had been drilled, the Powder Monkey put a charge of black powder into it and inserted a blasting cap. Electric wires were run from the cap along the ground for some distance and attached to a detonator. After making sure that everyone was well back from the site, Dad pushed the detonator plunger and, if everything had been done right, there was a dull roar from somewhere below and a lot of dust sifting up through cracks in various places. It really wasn't terribly complicated, once you knew what you were doing. At first, these detonations were major events for us kids, but they were nowhere near as rewarding as a giant explosion would have been and they soon became just one more step in what seemed to us like a never-ending process. As a result of the blast, a new batch of stone was now loose enough to pry out of the ground, load into the trailer and haul out. Mother and Dad were beginning to accumulate an impressive pile of stone up at the building site.

There was still no news about the working drawings, but we had been told Wright was at work on them. We assumed he was occupied with many projects and would finish our drawings in due course. Recently, I read Curtis Besinger's memoir of his years at the Taliesin Fellowship, *Working with Mr. Wright: What it was Like.* In the book he says,

> "Working by myself during the summer (1947), I did the working drawings for the Douglas Grant house in Cedar Rapids, Iowa. This was one of my favorite houses. It was essentially a simple house, but it had a spatial richness that was achieved in other houses only with a more complex form. Its construction and many of its details were similar to those of the Walter house (in Quasqueton, Iowa), so the drawings were done relatively easily." [9]

I found it interesting that Curtis Besinger did the drawings "relatively easily" in the summer of 1947, but that my parents didn't receive them until March of 1948. No wonder they couldn't understand what was taking so long. Mother and Dad exhibited a certain amount of naivety when they assumed Wright, himself, was doing the drawings; an assumption that no one at Taliesin did very much to dispel. Wright had a number of extremely talented apprentices at Taliesin who were every bit as capable of translating his designs into drawings as Wright himself—maybe better. It probably never occurred to my parents to wonder how Wright could have done the drawings for everything he was working on. The delay in timing, however, was due to the fact that Wright had to approve every drawing before he would sign it.

In doing research for the book, I have learned many things about our house that we never knew at the time. Usually, it has been something I uncovered while reading about Wright and the Fellowship, such as Besinger's comment about the working drawings. Sometimes it was a chance remark on the part of someone who knew Wright or worked with him. One such revelation came several years ago in New York City.

As I mentioned earlier, Wright told my parents in 1946 that he had already designed their house in his head. As it happened, however, it was not only in his head but it, or a house remarkably like it, was in his drafting room as well.

In July 1979 I went to see Edgar Kaufmann, Jr. in New York. Mr. Kaufmann studied with Wright, wrote extensively on his architecture and has included a fine description of the Grant house in his book, *Taliesin Drawings*. "Fallingwater", the magnificent house that Wright designed in 1935 for Kaufmann's parents near Mill Run, Pennsylvania, is one of the most dramatic examples of residential architecture in the world. Edgar Kaufmann, Jr. lived there for many years, and had been to visit my parents several times. He loved our house and often told Mother and Dad that he saw many similarities between it and "Fallingwater"; therefore, when I first began to think about writing a book about our house, I was anxious to talk to him.

We had a delightful conversation one afternoon at his apartment in New York. Over tea, we compared anecdotes about leaking roofs and problems with large glass windows and, although I was very much in awe of this man and his exquisite art collection, I found him to be warm and gracious; I was grateful that he had been kind enough to spend this time with me. At one point in our conversation, he suddenly said to me,

"You know, of course, about the other house?" I must have looked as confused and surprised as I felt, for he went on to say,

"Yes, Mr. Wright designed a house for some clients—I can't recall their name—about the same time, or possibly after, he designed

"Fallingwater". The house was never built, but your parents' house is quite similar in design."

Of course I had never heard of another house like ours and when I mentioned the conversation to my father, he was as surprised as I had been. Mr. Kaufmann was Director of Industrial Design at the Museum of Modern Art in New York from 1946-1955 and he suggested I talk to Arthur Drexler who now held that position. The museum has some Wright drawings in its collection and Mr. Kaufmann thought the drawings he remembered might be part of the lot. Mr. Drexler responded quickly to my inquiry with some surprising information:

"... we have ... two plans of a house for Mr. and Mrs. Stuart Wells ... dated 1946 ... the Wells drawings most certainly resemble the Grant house."

I found this information quite unsettling, but assumed that any similarity was due to the fact that the designs were both "Usonian" and obviously done at about the same time. However, when I saw the drawings of the Wells house, at Mr. Drexler's invitation, I could no longer attribute any similarity to coincidence; there was no doubt that the two designs were nearly identical.

The Wells and the Grant designs are so similar that the differences become interesting. Nearly all the differences in the Grant house are explained by specific requests by my parents, which Wright had obligingly worked into the existing design. The brick of the Wells house was changed to stone; the terraces were altered slightly to reflect the apparent differences in the terrain. The Wells master bedroom overlooked the living room and occupied a larger area than the corresponding space in the Grant house. The Grant master bedroom is located on the opposite side of the house—in accordance with Mother and Dad's wish to be as far as possible from the central living space. The space overlooking the living room in the Grant house is my bedroom and, while comparing the two designs, I may have stumbled upon the solution to something that had always mystified us: the fireplace in my bedroom. When our working drawings arrived, there was no longer a fireplace there. It's entirely possible that Wright simply forgot to eliminate the fireplace in that room when he reworked the Wells design to produce the Grant house. I prefer to think he left it there purposely, knowing it wouldn't be practical (there wouldn't have been room for a bed) but remembering a child's request for a fireplace in her room.

As I sat there by myself in the MOMA basement, studying the design that had so clearly preceded ours, I became uncomfortably aware that I was sorry I had uncovered this remarkable piece of information after all these years. I really felt a little cheated by the discovery that our design was a bit second-hand but, at the same time, I had to admire Wright for his practicality and single-minded objectivity. He was in the business of designing houses that would get built! Recently, during a visit to Taliesin West, I discussed this discovery with Bruce Brooks Pfeiffer, Director of Archives at the Wright Foundation. Bruce told me that, not only was the Wells house like the Grant house, but there was a third one—a house designed for Dr. and Mrs. Charles Bell in East St. Louis, Illinois; and, like the Wells design, it was never built. It is even more like the Grant house than the Wells design and it, too, has a fireplace in the bedroom overlooking the living room. So which one did Wright use when he worked on our house? Both of these designs deviated from the standard Usonian, in that they were on two levels. Both designs had been done for houses that were to be situated on a hillside and, when the Grant site turned out to be a hillside, too ... as Bruce put it, "Mr. Wright never liked to waste a drawing."

John Sergeant, in his book, *Frank Lloyd Wright's Usonian Houses*, says,

"Wright himself always gave exacting and personal attention to his clients, but they were more likely to get, indeed to request, a variation on a published or cancelled previous project. Those most likely to inspire him in his old, but incisive, age were those for whom the building would be a financial sacrifice, a continuing lifetime project, or a personal building activity." [10]

Perhaps that is the reason why Mother and Dad always found Wright so approachable and delightful to work with.

The Grant house is, after all, the one that was built; and the discovery that its beautiful design sprang into the mind of its creator on that October afternoon in 1946 with a little less spontaneity than we had always believed does nothing to diminish the pleasure it has given my family over the years. I do have to smile, though, each time I remember the serene assurance with which Wright announced to my parents, "I have already designed your house."

EIGHT

Drawings

On January 22, 1948, Dad wrote to Wright: "What is your candid opinion on the chances of our starting to build our house this year?"

Wright's answer, dated January 27: "Dear Grant: ... Candidly I wouldn't—for a year." [11]

There is no ready explanation for Wright's answer. In all probability he knew that, in the aftermath of World War II, building material such as structural steel was unobtainable, or at least in short supply, at the time. He may also have known that Mother and Dad would need a lot of time to quarry enough stone to keep the stone masons supplied once building began. Although they were anxious to get started on the house, they also were realistic; they resigned themselves to waiting for a year.

On March 16, 1948, the working drawings were sent, along with a bill for services in the amount of $1,000. Penned on the bottom of the bill: "Dear Grant—Herewith the 'sorrowful'. F.L.L.W." [12]

Dad's reply, dated March 22,

"The 'sorrowful' is not really sorrowful because we are so completely happy with the plans. Enclosed is our check.

"May we have the original sketches, too? (the preliminary drawings)? Not all of our friends can read blueprints and the Architectural Forum issue is sold out (the January 1948 issue).

"Words are inadequate to express the satisfaction we feel about the house you have designed for us. I suppose you have heard that many times before, but we want you to know that there is at least one family out in Cedar Rapids, Iowa which you have made very happy."

April 2nd, from Wright:

"Dear Douglas Grant: Thank you. We are glad to know the Grants are 'at home'.

"The original sketches are the property of the architect but we will send copies. Meanwhile we are mailing a copy of the Forum." [13]

The Grant house was included in the January 1948 Forum, with a reproduction of the preliminary sketch for the south view of the house and the floor plans for both levels. Curiously, the text describes chimneys and terrace walls made of brick—either an error on someone's part or some confusion about which set of plans they were looking at.

You may wonder why Dad was so persistent about asking for the preliminary drawings. As I mentioned earlier, they were extremely attractive. The drawing of the south view, with its long expanse of stone and concrete culminating in the two-story glass living room, was particularly stunning. In March 2007, when my husband and I visited Taliesin West in Scottsdale, Arizona, Bruce Pfeiffer had assembled all of the original drawings—early sketches, preliminary drawings and the full set of working drawings with details, in anticipation of our visit. Seeing those drawings again after all these years brought back a flood of memories and reinforced my conviction that they were particularly well drawn.

Bruce told me that he was almost certain the preliminary drawings had been done by John DeKoven Hill. John Hill was the Taliesin senior apprentice assigned by Wright to supervise the construction of our house, and we saw a great deal of him during those years. He was the one who helped solve problems as they occurred and answered questions that inevitably arose about various aspects of the construction process. Bruce told us that John was always extraordinarily precise in his drawing, but always bemoaned the fact that he couldn't draw trees. The trees in the Grant drawings are lightly rendered, mere suggestions of trees, which give the work an almost Japanese print quality. I wish we'd known that John was the artist. He came to Cedar Rapids a year or two before Mother died, to see her and perhaps to renew old memories. It was a nostalgic visit, and David told me they talked at length about many things. It's not surprising that the subject of the drawings didn't come up then but, if it had, would John have finally told us? Bruce Pfeiffer also told me that day at Taliesin West that Edgar Kaufmann, Jr. had been so fond of the drawing of the south view of the Grant house that he commissioned another one for his own collection.

Wright told Dad he would send copies of the drawings, but he never did. In September 1983, while my husband and I were living in New York City, we read that the Max Protetch Gallery was proposing to sell 100 of Wright's drawings from the archives of the Frank Lloyd Wright Foundation. I called the gallery, explained my interest in the drawings and asked if, by some chance, there was a drawing of the Grant house in the lot. I was told that indeed there was; it was the drawing of the south perspective. As we set out for the gallery that weekend, my husband and I discussed the fact that my parents had never received copies of the drawings. Wouldn't it be wonderful if we could purchase this drawing and give it to them? We had no idea what price was being asked, and we had a very limited budget, but we resolved to give it a try. We established a price beyond which we would not go and hoped for the best. The drawing was not among those on display at the gallery but, when I expressed a desire to see it and told them my connection with it, Max Protetch ushered us into a back room and it was brought out for viewing.

Seeing the drawing again after 36 years was an emotional experience for me and, frankly, I was more than a little upset by the circumstances under which I was given the opportunity. It felt wrong to see these drawings up for sale. When the staff learned that my parents had built the house, were living in it still and that I had met Wright on more than one occasion, they bombarded me with questions. We talked for quite a long time about the house and what it was like to work with Wright, but finally we got around to the subject of purchasing the drawing. When we finally ventured to ask the price, the answer came back quickly—$40,000. Gulp! That was considerably higher than we were prepared to go, and we reluctantly passed on the offer. Mr. Protetch cleverly commented, "That's probably more than your father paid for the house!"

I expressed surprise that the price was so high; it was a lovely drawing, but this was hardly "Fallingwater". On the other hand, I felt some comfort in the fact that it might not be sold to anyone for the same reason. I was concerned about what would happen to it if it didn't sell, and was told that it would be returned to the archives at Taliesin in that event. And so it was. Shortly after that experience, Bruce Pfeiffer thoughtfully arranged to have a photo-montage of the drawing made for me, and it is a treasured part of our art collection. We finally met up with the original again on March 14, 2007, at Taliesin West. I was glad to see it again, and I am happy that it's there. If we are not to have it, then that is where it belongs.

NINE

A Good Stonemason

On June 22, 1948, Dad wrote to Wright, telling him they were pleased with the way the stone quarry was working out. He said that he and Mother had already taken out a large quantity of excellent building stone and they felt there was an unlimited supply in the quarry which was easily available. He expressed his concern about finding a reliable stonemason who would take on the job. There were several in the area who had been recommended, but Dad had not contacted any of them yet. I believe he was hoping that Wright would be able to suggest someone, particularly since the Miller house, which was ninety miles away in Charles City, had in all probability employed local stonemasons. Also, Dad was uncertain about what size stone they should be accumulating; he thought perhaps a stonemason might provide some guidance in that area. Finally, he told Wright that he and Mother were impatient to get started building. Was there any chance they could begin work on the house in the near future? Should he begin to get tentative estimates from local subcontractors and building material sources, or was this something that Wright preferred to handle? Wright replied that he couldn't imagine where all the good stonemasons were hiding, but he implied that finding one was up to us.

Finding a good stonemason was not going to be easy. Most of the local stonemasons were accustomed to working stone in quite a different way from what would be required here and were, frankly, not interested. Again it was our friend, Ron Henderson, who came to the rescue. He knew Dad was looking for a mason and he called one day to say,

> "I was eating lunch the other day in a local restaurant and I heard these guys discussing stone. I'd never heard anybody talk about stone the way this one guy did. He described it like it was something fine, like silk, that you had to treat with respect. So I went over to him and told him about you and your house, and told him you were looking for a stonemason. His name is Bob Cooper and I've got his telephone number for you."

Bob Cooper was unquestionably the man for the job. Dad liked him right away and, when he described the kind of stone work that would be required, Bob said he could do that. What is more, he had learned to read blueprints while serving in the army and he could be ready to start whenever we were ready for him. Could Dad supply him with enough stone to keep him busy?

Mother and Dad now quarried with a vengeance. They worked harder than ever before, now that their goal was in sight. They had worked out a routine: Dad got up about 5:00 in the morning, went down and got out a load of stone and brought it up to the site in the trailer. He then bathed and dressed and went to work at the radio station. During school vacations, Mother assigned us our household tasks for the morning and then took her turn in the quarry, bringing up another load. During the school year, she got us off to school first (there were no school busses; we walked) and then she went to the quarry. When Dad came home for lunch, he helped her unload the stone. After he went back to work, she did another stint, bringing up another trailer-load which Dad helped her unload when he got home in the evening. We ate our evening meal promptly at 5:30, which meant there were still several hours of daylight left before the sun went down, at least in the summer months. So, back to the quarry they went. Sometimes just Dad went in the evening; Mother needed some time to catch up with household chores. But often Mother went with him to bring up one more load of stone before dark. When school was out for the summer, I like to think that I was a great help around the house; I was thirteen by this time. I probably didn't contribute much to the smooth running of the household, though. Oh, I was able to keep my brother and sister from killing each other when Mother was at the quarry; but we were actually pretty good kids and Mother could trust us to manage without her for a while. The truth is, I don't really know how Mother and Dad kept up the frantic pace they set for themselves. I do know, however, that there wasn't an ounce of fat on either of them! When I think back to that time when the quarry work was so intense, I suppose the obsession with piling up stone was explained by their frustration at not yet being able to start the house. At least it was something they could do!

The quarry site had a lot of charm at certain times of the year. In the spring there were many wildflowers to be found, and in the fall the foliage was spectacular and there were wild blackberries to be picked. But in summer it was not a pleasant place to be. It was located in the creek bottom land, where very little air moved to cool it off. It was understandably damp down there and, as a result, the mosquito population was an extremely vigorous one. The mosquitoes might have been the size of eagles for all the damage they did. The only mosquito repellant we had was not very effective against these monsters. Dad always maintained they didn't bother him, and I admit he is the only person I have ever known who didn't swell up and itch when mosquitoes went to work on him.

Mother and Dad would continue to quarry stone long after the building started, and would keep on doing so throughout the construction process. Once the stonemasons started work, the need for stone was so great that there were times when they weren't sure they could keep up with the unrelenting demand. They were determined, though, that progress on the house would not be held up by anything they could control, and so they returned again and again to what must sometimes have seemed to be a Sisyphean task they had set for themselves.

By the time Mother and Dad finally started construction, they were almost totally focused on one thing alone—getting the house built. Soon they would contribute nearly every available minute to building the house, and they would find themselves almost totally engaged in meeting the many challenges it presented. Perhaps it was then that the house began to take on a life of its own, a life that would eventually assume an importance that no one could have imagined.

TEN

Construction Begins

In the fall of 1948 Mother and Dad made another journey to Wisconsin; they had many things to discuss with Wright. It would soon become necessary for Dad to set about the job of ordering building material, but there were several unanswered questions about what some of that material would be. These questions needed to be addressed, since there was some uncertainty about what was available and quite a bit of concern about the costs involved. David, Linda and I went along on this trip to Taliesin, since Wright still seemed eager to include the children in these visits, as well as the adults. We drove up on a Sunday, and this time we stayed for dinner. Sunday evening dinners, as I have mentioned before, were a very important part of the ritual at Taliesin. They were typically attended by Mr. and Mrs. Wright and family, the Fellowship and invited guests, which sometimes included celebrities from many different professions. Individual tables were placed around the large living room, with Mr. and Mrs. Wright at a larger table, in close proximity to everyone else. The meal was served by the architectural apprentices, who had also cooked the food and would wash the dishes afterward. We children were expected to be on our very best behavior that night: only the best table manners, eat everything on our plates and no fighting. I don't remember everything about the evening, but I do recall that we were so completely impressed by the surroundings and the whole atmosphere of the place that there was no question of anything but exemplary behavior from any of us. In fact, we may not have said a word all evening! I remember that the food was not very good—overcooked meat and undercooked carrots, but we ate it all without a murmur. After dinner, the tables were cleared away and everyone found seats around the room for the music performance, a long-standing Sunday evening tradition at Taliesin.

The programs were originally planned by Mrs. Wright's daughter, Svetlana, who played a leading role in the Taliesin music scene. She was married to senior Fellowship architect, Wesley Peters, and was a great favorite of everyone at Taliesin. She was an accomplished musician, who played both piano and violin. But she and her younger son, Daniel, had died the previous fall in a tragic automobile accident, and the Taliesin community was still grieving her death. Now the programs were planned and performed by the Fellowship architects, most of whom were also talented musicians. It was not unusual for visiting professional musicians to perform at these affairs on occasion, but Wright really preferred the home-grown music produced by his group at Taliesin.

I don't know what was performed that evening, but my brother, David, was totally smitten by Mr. and Mrs. Wright's daughter, Iovanna, who played the harp. He talked about her all the way home that night and vowed to marry her when he grew up, in spite of the fact that she was 25 and he was not quite eight. As we said our goodbyes and expressed our pleasure at being included in the evening's festivities, Mrs. Wright seemed to genuinely regret that we would not be spending the night. But, enchanted as we were with Taliesin hospitality, reality prevailed. Dad had to work the next day and we had to go to school.

During that visit to Taliesin, Wright told Dad that he'd considered substituting a wooden roof for the concrete slab called for in the working drawings. That was a major change, to say the least, and I have no idea what prompted it. But, as a result, Dad was understandably anxious to settle the matter and get on with the business of ordering lumber. At the end of March 1949, Dad wrote to Wright, following up on many of the things they had discussed. Wright had suggested that Dad might investigate the possibility of buying a full carload of either redwood or cypress. It had taken Dad a long time to get the information he needed, but now he had something to report:

"First of all, redwood seems pretty much out of the picture in this part of the country. It's still scarce and prices are fantastically high. The cypress picture is much better. A friend of ours in the lumber business (honest, reliable) can get a carload of rough-sawn, tidewater red cypress, one-inch planks, and will deliver it to our site for $135 per thousand ..."

Dad addressed Wright's suggestion that he buy random thicknesses of lumber, re-sawing it to fit our requirements, by reporting that he had investigated that possibility and concluded that it would result in very little savings and a great deal more effort. He implored Wright to let him know if he intended to revise the plans and substitute a wooden roof for the concrete slab that was currently specified. This was information he needed as soon as possible, since the change would result in a vastly different estimate of the quantity of lumber that would be required for the house. He was being pressed by the lumber company to give them as much time as possible to order, and he also thought it would be necessary to get the lumber on site early enough to stack it and let it dry before construction began.

And, while he was on the subject of wood, he asked Wright why it wouldn't make sense to use the same cypress for the interior partitions, cupboards, shelves and wardrobe drawers. In fact why not use cypress for window and door frames instead of the expensive steel that was specified? This was something that Dad could build himself, saving a great deal of money in the process. He also told Wright at this time that he was planning to do all of the electric wiring and some of the plumbing himself, saying, "I figure that in this case I'm probably more valuable as a plumber than as a radio broadcaster."

Finally, he closed by saying, "… at this moment our house looks much nearer to reality than ever before and we're all getting pretty excited."

At this point, Wright was traveling to various places, including San Francisco and New York, and was apparently not available to provide Dad with immediate answers to his questions. There is nothing in the correspondence to indicate that Wright either approved or disapproved of Dad's suggestions, or how the roof became concrete again instead of wood, but everything seems to have been sorted out by the time construction started in October. David and I believe they must have conducted many of their conversations by telephone; it was probably rather expensive, but it would have saved a great deal of time.

In retrospect, Dad was extremely fortunate to have been able to get the lumber he needed at such a good price. In *Frank Lloyd Wright, The Masterworks,* Bruce Brooks Pfeiffer says,

> "By the time that the William Palmer house and the Isadore Zimmerman house were being built, in the early 1950's, it was apparent to Wright that the Usonian building system as described in 1938 was no longer cost-effective. Red tidewater cypress, the beautiful honey gold wood that Wright favored, had become scarce and costly." [14]

In October 1949, excavation for the house started at last; Ron Henderson began bulldozing out the space that would become the utility area. Usonian houses typically have no basements but, since this house was to fit right into the hill, the area underground would be used for the furnace and water heater, laundry room, preserved food storage and Dad's photographic dark room. The area would be accessed through the kitchen and by the outside door that my parents had asked Wright to add to the original design. Instead of poured footings, ditches four feet deep were dug; crushed rock was added and tamped down with a compressed air vibrator. These ditches, topped with poured concrete, would be the underpinnings for the stone walls to come. The living room's design made it appear to be soaring out of the hillside; consequently, it was quite a distance above ground level at the opposite end. Concrete was poured for the wall below the far end of the living room and the wall around the north terrace. Stone would be laid up against the outside of these walls at a later date. Finally, dirt was filled into the space created by these concrete walls up to the level of the future living room floor. Now it was time to begin thinking about building the stone walls.

Dad wrote to Wright on October 26, 1949,

"I'm enclosing a couple of photos of our sample wall which John Hill suggested I send you. This wall wasn't laid up any too carefully, and we experimented with many different kinds and sizes of stone in a small area. Even so, we think the wall presents a very attractive face, and with a few minor improvements, would work into the house very well. I hope you concur and that you can get a fairly accurate idea of how it looks from the pictures.

"Excavation for the house is nearly done. It has slowed down over the past week or so because of a brief flurry of illness which put Mrs. Grant in the hospital for several days (she had infectious mononucleosis; small wonder). Because of this, and a brief bout with the flu which I had, we were unable to give the project our full attention. Now, happily, we all are on the mend, and I have hopes that we'll be ready to pour concrete within a few days ..."

As mentioned previously, John DeKoven Hill, one of the senior apprentices, had been assigned by Wright to be Dad's liaison with Taliesin while the house was under construction. That relationship was to be an enormously important one. Not only was John easy to work with and enjoyable to be around, but he had a unique ability to read Wright's mind when necessary. When I asked Dad once if he thought Wright did a good job of answering the many questions Dad put to him during construction of the house, he replied that Wright often answered by recounting experiences he had had in the past. Sometimes his musings were genuinely interesting, but not terribly helpful for the problem

Air compressor used in blasting out the stone.

Photo of the sample wall Dad built to send to Wright. He placed the shovel on top to indicate the scale, but apparently Wright missed that detail.

at hand. At these times, John Hill always seemed to know what Wright wanted done, and he was able to save a lot of time as well as prevent several unfortunate errors along the way. This proved to be more important than anyone could have ever imagined at the time construction was just beginning.

During the winter of 1949-50, the concrete wall between the kitchen and utility area was poured and work began on the stone walls. Several months before, Dad had come up with a method to lay the stone in forms of his own design. These slip-forms were light enough to be moved up as work progressed, and they made it possible for the stone walls to appear the way Wright wanted them—no mortar showing on the face of the stone. Nearly all stone walls in the house, both exterior and interior, were double, with stone on both sides; therefore, it was necessary to design a form that would accomplish this by allowing both sides to be built at the same time. Dad's form consisted of two rectangular sides of wood

Forms that Dad invented in place on the walls.

planking, open on both ends, with no top or bottom, held together with metal strapping that could be adjusted to accommodate varying wall thicknesses. Each stone was chipped to produce one reasonably straight edge, if it didn't have one naturally, and laid inside the form in stratified layers—resembling the way stone is found in the ground—with the straight or "good" edge up against each side so it would be facing out when the form was moved up. Since each stone varied in thickness and shape, the face that showed provided a texture that was pleasantly uneven. Mortar was then filled into the space between the two stone walls and left to cure overnight. The next day, the form was moved up to the top of the new wall and the process began again. The design was flexible enough to permit the forms to curve when a curve was called for, yet rigid when straight walls were needed. Specifications called for the outside walls to incorporate a two-inch "dead air" space, which was

Construction of the living room pier and north wall. View to the north. Phil Feddersen

meant to serve as insulation. As the stone was laid in the form, a separate device consisting of two boards, two inches apart, was inserted in the middle of the form and moved up at the same time. Material for the forms was simple: ordinary wooden planks, with metal strapping and levers attached to allow the forms to be tightened in place. Bob Cooper salvaged the metal required from discarded farm windmill parts.

In his book, *Frank Lloyd Wright's Usonian Houses,* John Sergeant remarks,

> "The Grants ... evolved a method of laying (the stone) up in boxes, with concrete to the rear, in a way not dissimilar to that used by the Nearings in Vermont." [15]

He was referring to Scott and Helen Nearing who, in their book, *Living the Good Life,* described the stone house they constructed in Winhall, Vermont.[16] Dad would have been fascinated to know that the Nearings

South balcony with dining room planting box below. Phil Feddersen

had used forms to build up the walls of their house at roughly the same time he was doing the same thing. The forms, as described in the Nearing book, appear to be somewhat different; they were not building the same kind of stone walls. But the Nearing book was not published until 1954, and I don't think Dad ever read it.

Bob Cooper hired a crew of four workmen to help him build the stone walls: Don Scheer, Kenny Lahue, Melvin (Johnny) Timms and Larry Christianson. These men were farmers, not builders, and it's a credit to them and to Bob Cooper that they were able to learn a new skill so quickly. It's entirely possible that one reason they learned so quickly was that they had no previous stone laying technique to "unlearn". During that winter they laid the stone for the dining room pier, the north wall, the dining room "planting box", the dining room and living room fireplaces, and the great pier on the north side of the living room—all up to the level where the second floor would begin. The winter was a reasonably mild one for Iowa, and the masons were able to work through it without many interruptions due to weather. To keep themselves warm while they worked on the walls, and to help dry out the mortar, they made an enclosure out of canvas tarpaulins and heated the space they created with a kerosene "salamander", or portable stove. The enclosure also served as a way to keep the newly laid mortar from freezing, so they left the salamander burning when they went home at the end of the day. On one occasion, however, the wind picked up during the night and blew the tarpaulin against the stove, where it eventually caught fire and burned, along with the wooden form they were using. Fortunately, all they lost was a tarpaulin, some of the scaffolding and a portion of the wooden forms. Those could be replaced, and the black soot cleaned off the stone, but the incident served as an incentive to perfect the design for the stove's enclosure!

In December 1949, Dad and Mother took some time off and we drove to California to have Christmas with Grandpa and Grandma Grant, who had moved there to escape the Iowa winters. We arranged to pay a call at Taliesin West in Scottsdale, Arizona on the way back; there were some matters Dad wanted to discuss with Wright in person. The visit would also be a great treat for us, since David and Linda had never been West before.

At that time, Taliesin West was truly a desert retreat. It lay far beyond the outskirts of Phoenix, and Scottsdale was a very small town. Having spent our entire lives in the Midwest, we found the desert to be an exotic landscape, and we could hardly wait to get out of the car and walk around in it. Taliesin was a camp in the desert, albeit a rather luxurious one by most standards. It was a cluster of low-lying buildings that blended in beautifully with the surrounding landscape, largely due to the native stone of which they were made, but also because the lines of the structures themselves echoed the lines of the hills behind them. Taliesin West looked as if it had always been there.

I don't recall who met us when we arrived, but we were greeted with great enthusiasm and made to feel completely welcome. It was explained that Mr. Wright was in the midst of a meeting, but Senior Architect, Wes Peters, would be happy to talk with Dad about several building matters. Afterward, we would be given a tour of the premises while we waited for Mr. Wright.

My memory is far from complete concerning the details of that tour, but a few things stand out. There was a shallow reflecting pool near the entrance, and near the pool were large, flat metal trays overflowing with grapefruit. We were told that a local farmer had recently lost a great deal of fruit from his trees due to a windstorm, so he invited the Fellowship to come and take as much as they wanted. Grapefruit was considered an occasional treat in our household and, seeing it in such abundance was almost more than we could handle. I remember the living room as being a large, dramatic space with colorful accents in the form of cushions and woven throws. The light in this room was a welcome retreat from the bright desert sun, since it was greatly diffused by white canvas panels stretched across a wooden framework that served as the roof. There was a large concert grand piano at one end of the room and seating in the form of low chairs and benches. It looked luxuriously comfortable.

After all that comfort, the guest rooms were a remarkable contrast. They were arranged in a row along an outside balcony, with only a heavy curtain between the room and the elements. They were little more than monk-like cells with beds, and we could not help but wonder if guests were welcome here for very long. Granted, the desert climate is a predominantly warm one; however, nights can be very cold at times. Well, it was, after all, a camp in the desert.

When we returned to the main courtyard, Wright was still engaged so we decided to take a walk in the surrounding desert. We were cautioned by one of the apprentices, as we were about to set out, not to get too close to a certain variety of cactus, known colloquially as the "jumping cactus", because sections of it break off and attach themselves to whatever has touched them, and contact with the barbs is extremely painful. We enjoyed our walk, exploring this environment which was so new to us. David and Linda had a great time shoving each other into the sand and other juvenile pursuits that I was too old and sophisticated, at fourteen, to indulge in. All went well until Mother apparently got too close to what was undoubtedly a "jumping cactus". She was wearing a jacket with a belt that hung loose on either side, and the belt must have brushed against the cactus. As a result, a sizeable chunk of cactus "jumped" on to one end of her belt. The next thing we knew, our mother had been attacked by a cactus; the chunk was now firmly attached to her hand and it was very painful. Dad suggested we go back to Taliesin for help, but Mother, too mortified to admit what had happened, insisted that Dad should try to extract it. He did have his nail clipper with him and, after some deft but painful maneuvering, he managed to get it off and to remove most of the barbs from her hand. On the way back, Mother made us all promise we wouldn't tell anyone at Taliesin about the cactus incident.

Wright was now free, so Mother and Dad went in to talk with him. It never occurred to us to wonder what they were discussing; probably more stuff about the house which was, frankly, not all that interesting to us. The three of us were left in the courtyard to entertain ourselves, so we began to look around to see what was available. David suggested we help ourselves to grapefruit; he had found a wastebasket with a knife in it, which suggested to him that grapefruit eating was encouraged. Linda didn't think we were supposed to, but David convinced her that it would be perfectly all right. I was at that age when almost everything is embarrassing; the thought of making an error in judgment involving grapefruit, or anything else for that matter, was a deciding factor in my decision to pass it up. Anyway, I thought this would be an excellent opportunity to continue work on the suntan I had started in California, with which I planned to impress my friends at home. David went to work right away on the grapefruit, and he and Linda shared one, and then another of the delicious yellow bounty. It was when he was contemplating a third that the meeting broke up and Wright appeared with Mother and Dad. Apparently Wright assessed the situation accurately, because he said to David, "I wouldn't eat too many of those if I were you."

Much to my parents' discomfort, David answered, "Why?"

"Because if you eat too many grapefruit you will have to go to the bathroom a great deal, and you have a very long car trip ahead of you."

With this, we were hustled quickly into the car. Before leaving, however, Dad stayed behind for a few more words with Wright. When he returned to the car, we all said our goodbyes and left Taliesin West for the drive home. We drove on for a time before anyone said anything. Then Mother said, "How did it go?'

Dad replied, "Well, we exchanged a few pleasantries, and then I said to him,

'Mr. Wright, I know we still owe you the last installment of your fee, and I apologize for not getting it to you yet.'

"He stopped me, saying, 'I appreciate your bringing it up, but don't worry about it.'

"I said, 'I don't understand.'

"And then he said, 'There was a time when I really needed the money, but I don't need it now. Why don't you wait until you've made a lot of money in your broadcasting business and then donate the fee to the Foundation.'

"And that was the way we left it."

ELEVEN

Many Questions

By early 1950, the construction process was beginning to move more quickly, and Dad had many questions for the architects at Taliesin. Some of them had to do with the big vertical steel support beams, or mullions, that were an integral part of the design. Dad was getting ready to place an order for the steel, but he was having difficulty figuring out exactly what was specified on the working drawings in a couple of instances. He wrote to John Hill in January asking for clarification as soon as possible.

I'm sure there were times during the building process when Dad must have felt a somewhat frightening amount of inadequacy for the task at hand. There must have been moments when he feared he had taken on more than he was capable of doing. However, it was too late to change at this point, and it was against Dad's nature to give up when things were difficult. It's also possible that there were some areas of the drawings where details were vague on the assumption that the reader's grasp of the design was more sophisticated than was actually the case; Wright typically expected a great deal from his building contractors. In any case, Dad apparently got the answers he need from John Hill by telephone, since there is nothing in the correspondence. Ever optimistic, Dad ended his letter to John by saying,

"Work is progressing quite fast. The entire double fireplace has been constructed up to the ceiling line and most of the north wall is almost done. Looks good to us. Hope Mr. Wright will like it."

As construction was in high gear by this time, there were many more questions. Most of them were answered by John Hill, and most of the correspondence at this point was with him. However, on February 11, Dad wrote to Wright with a question about the top surfaces, or copings, for the outside stone walls, some of which would be exposed to the weather; and he offered a possible alternative method for constructing the recessed light boxes which would be embedded in the ceilings. The drawings showed the copings to be made of stone about six inches thick. The problem was that none of our stone was suitable for this purpose because most of it was much thinner than that. Thicker stone from nearby quarries was too soft to withstand harsh weather. Dad suggested they might make the copings out of concrete, cast in place on the walls. What did Wright think of that idea?

It occurred to Dad that the light receptacles, which were to be boxes made of sheet iron and recessed into the ceiling, could just as easily be made without the iron. Wooden forms could be made at the time the ceiling was poured, leaving box-shaped receptacles with outlet boxes in place. They were to be painted the same color as the ceilings, anyway, and it would save the cost of fabricating special metal boxes. Was Wright agreeable to that suggestion?

Once again, Dad urged Wright to provide him with the revised details for the interior wooden partitions because he needed to order the lumber. He finished his letter, saying,

"We have made much greater progress on the job during the winter months than I had ever imagined would be possible. At the present rate we expect to begin forming for the first floor slab within the next few weeks."

Apparently Dad's suggestion for making the wall copings of cast concrete was not met with enthusiasm at Taliesin, probably for aesthetic reasons. John Hill replied on February 20th that the stone walls must have a stone coping and that it might be possible to find stone that would work from some of the sandstone quarries along the Mississippi. The texture might be different, but it was more important to have the color match our walls. Wright approved Dad's idea for forming the light boxes, as long as care was taken to do a neat job.

According to the original specifications for the house, the concrete slab roof was to have a stamped copper facia trim all around the edge, similar to that used at Florida Southern College in Lakeland, Florida. Indeed, the description of the Grant house in the 1948 *Architectural Forum* included a reference to the copper facias. The copper would oxidize over time into a shade of turquoise green and was to be a striking architectural detail of the house. Dad repeatedly asked to be sent drawings and specifications for the facia trim so that he could begin to get price quotes, but none were forthcoming until June 1950 when the company that fabricated the trim for Florida Southern College sent him samples and prices. To his horror, Dad realized that the facia would add $10,000 to the cost of the house. He simply could not afford to do it; he could think of no more places where he could cut costs on the house in order to accommodate that price. Regretfully, he broke the news to Wright that it would not be possible to include the copper trim. Wright seemed to take it in stride, although he was undoubtedly disappointed. It would have been a beautiful addition to the house, and I still get questions about it on the very few occasions when I talk to anyone who was involved with the design.

But apparently Wright understood the situation, and knew that Dad had made the only decision he could. He changed the specifications to incorporate a facia made entirely of concrete.

The next set of problems involved the steel casement windows and doors, none of which were in stock sizes. Dad wrote to John Hill on March 15, 1950,

> "I'm running into a lot of trouble in trying to get steel casement windows and doors in the sizes specified … Neither (the brand specified) nor two or three other manufacturers carry stock sizes anywhere near the sizes specified … Also, all our inquiries so far result in offers of multi-pane windows; nobody has the single-pane frames we need.
>
> "None of the concerns contacted are willing to manufacture special sizes. Apparently they have all the business they can handle on their regular stock items. I have one more possibility. I've just learned of a small company in Dubuque which may be able to make the sizes we need to order. We are contacting them immediately and should know in another week. But even if they are willing to make them to order, I'm afraid the price may be sky-high.
>
> "As I see it, there is one alternative. How about making the windows and doors out of cypress similar to the interior partitions? I can get them made to fit, with narrow frames, etc. at a fairly reasonable price. I'd appreciate it if you would discuss this with Mr. Wright at your earliest convenience and let me know as soon as possible."

It is interesting to note that Wright had originally intended for his Usonian houses to feature components that would be readily available. To quote Bruce Brooks Pfeiffer,

"He (Wright) had first experimented in prefabricated housing in 1915-1917 for a project he called 'The American Ready-Cut System', in which all the lumber and millwork pieces were to be precut in a factory, shipped to the site, and assembled. The idea was precocious, and the system never flourished. But in the Usonian houses he returned to the idea of a system that could be easily adapted to factory technology." [17]

Apparently, World War II changed all that.

John Hill's letter of March 22 brought the welcome news that Wright approved the cypress sashes if the metal ones could not be made. He asked if Dad had had any luck finding stone for the wall copings and requested some photos of the work so far, if possible.

And still more problems. To John Hill on March 25,

"Two more problems. First, we can't seem to reconcile the upper level and the lower level floor plans on unit line E between lines 10 and 14. Is the masonry wall on the upper level supposed to project beyond the lower level wall into the stairway at this point? Perhaps you can send us a drawing that will clear this up."

In his book, *Working with Mr. Wright*, Curtis Besinger says,

"Mr. Wright insisted that we (the Taliesin architects) made too many drawings, that there was no need to detail all of the special conditions. He said that a good builder should be able to understand the grammar of a house's construction and would be able to work out these special conditions, as and where they occurred." [18]

There is no question that Dad was struggling to fulfill his self-appointed role as General Contractor, and I doubt if he would have characterized himself as "a good builder" at times when he thought he was in over his head. It was hard enough trying to interpret the blueprints without being called upon to "understand the grammar of the house's construction" and to work out the "special conditions" they encountered on occasion. With everything now going on at full steam, there were bound to be some slip-ups. The letter to John Hill continues in a tone so seemingly calm and offhand that the full significance of its message isn't immediately grasped:

"Second, we have just discovered a mistake we made in the footing for the west wall to the living room and terrace…In some way we have placed this footing four inches closer to unit line 1, in other words, 4 inches off center. As you may recall, this is a 12 inch concrete wall which is some 10 feet high at the northwest corner. We intend to face it with stone on the outside for a total thickness of 16 inches. It would be a major project to try and change it now.

"Would it be possible to simply make the living room 4 inches longer? As nearly as I can tell, this would involve only extending a few of the horizontal steel mullions and increasing the size of several sheets of glass by four inches. It would leave the roof dimension unchanged. Another alternative might be moving the mullions inward four inches off center, thus leaving the room dimensions unchanged. We'll appreciate your ideas on this little problem!"

The error was discovered by Dad and Bob Cooper, and I can only guess at the horror that Dad must have felt as its full significance began to dawn on him. He was going to have to tell Frank Lloyd Wright that he (Dad) had made a major building mistake in Wright's design for the house. "Little problem", indeed! Unfortunately, there is no record of how the problem was received at Taliesin, but no lightning bolts were hurled from on high, and it's entirely possible that Wright never learned of it. I do know that the living room is longer than the plans specified, but not more than about four inches. Apparently, this was one special condition that was worked out to everyone's satisfaction.

By the end of spring 1950, they had laid the stone for the living room west wall, below what would eventually be a large expanse of plate glass. Concrete was poured for the walls in the utility area and a layer of crushed rock put down as a base for all the downstairs floors. Since Dad was his own electrical sub-contractor, he laid the electrical conduit pipes and placed the outlets in the downstairs walls and on the floor base, and then pulled all the wiring through the conduit. In keeping with the way he learned most things, he taught himself to become an electrician. He had acquired a certain amount of experience when he and Mother built their first house, but he set about reading everything he could find on the subject and never hesitated to ask questions when there were things he didn't understand at first. He learned some things by trial and error, fortunately nothing that was irreparable or catastrophic. The first time he laid conduit in the stone walls, for example, he neglected to plug the ends temporarily and they promptly filled up with mortar when it was added to the forms.

However, he knew his limits when it came to plumbing. He had done a little of that before, but the plumbing requirements for this house were several levels above the simple installation of toilets and lava-tories, and would require an expertise not easily come by. The heating for the house was to be Wright's Gravity Heating system, comprised of pipes laid under the concrete and stone floors through which hot water flowed. The theory was that cold air would naturally gravitate down to the floors where it would be heated, rise again as warm air and eventu-ally heat the living space. Since the second story floors had heating pipes as well, a little of that heat would find its way down through the ceiling of the room below, adding to the allover warmth. It was a remarkable concept, and it made a great deal of sense. We had no way of knowing

Heating pipes for gravity heating in the living room.

then what adventures we would eventually have with Gravity Heating.

So Dad needed a good plumber. For many years he had been a member of the local school board, and later its president. While chairman of the building and grounds committee, he met a lot of contractors. He remembered one plumbing contractor who had impressed him with the quality of his workmanship, so Dad approached him with the idea of hiring him for the job he needed to fill. "Tex" Puth was enthusiastic when Dad described the situation, he loved the design of the house, and was quite capable of reading blueprints; he had gained his experience working in the Texas oil fields. There was never any doubt that he was our man. When the time came to lay out the wrought iron heating pipes on the crushed rock base of the floors, he knew exactly what he had to do. Wright was adamant about the specific brand of pipe he wanted, and would accept no substitutes; he had always had good luck with that particular piping and saw no reason to change. The specifications called for 2 ½-3" diameter pipes spaced about fourteen inches apart. Tex thought he could use 2" pipes, laid closer together, and achieve the same results.

By using the smaller diameter piping, he could save money by bending it himself in his own shop, rather than sending it out to be bent on the special equipment required for thicker pipe. He produced a series of shop drawings to illustrate his theory and they were submitted to Wright, who approved them.

Each day, David, Linda and I came home from school and ran down to the site to see what had been accomplished. In late afternoon and on weekends, when the work crew wasn't there, we wandered around in the future lower level trying to imagine what our house would really look like. It was a little easier now that there were partial walls and the two downstairs fireplaces. The living room fireplace was so big that we could all get into it with room to spare, and it was hard to believe this vast space would someday be a fireplace. We had only one small fireplace in our present house, but we all loved having a fire in cold weather and we spent many winter nights in front of the fireplace warming our backsides or making popcorn over the coals—a Sunday night ritual.

In May 1950 the work crew built the forms for the upstairs concrete floors, and the balcony floors and walls. Footings for the master bedroom, bath and locker room were dug, as these rooms were built on grade. A crushed rock base was laid in each room, steel mullions placed as required for support, and heating pipes laid out for the upper level floors. Plumbing for the bathrooms was installed and electrical conduit and outlets were placed on the floor base and up into the walls. On May 25 they poured the floor and the balcony from the west end of the house to the entrance loggia; the next day they did the remaining floors east of the loggia. The loggia floor would be finished with flagstone at a later date.

With so much happening at once now, the building site was an extremely busy place, with Mother and Dad, the stonemasons and their helpers, and the plumbing crew all occupied with their respective jobs. During the course of the house's construction, all of Bob Cooper's crew eventually bought new cars; evidently the Grant house was doing its part for the local economy. However, the builder's union was not quite so happy with the situation when it eventually came to their attention. The masons were non-union, in fact they were really farmers; union masons had not been interested in the job, because they didn't know how to lay stone as specified here. Tex Puth, the plumbing sub-contractor, and his men were union members; Dad was his own electrical contractor and was, of course, non-union. There was a great deal of grumbling at the Union Hall about this situation. Finally, Dad went to the Cedar Rapids Labor Council to try and persuade them it was all right, but doing so wasn't easy. The strongest protests came from the labor union, but they were able to work out a compromise: if Kenny Lahue (the "Mud Man", or the laborer who mixed the mortar and brought it to the stonemasons) joined the union, they would agree to the arrangement. Dad gladly paid Kenny's union dues for the duration of the construction.

At this point, one has to wonder if the Do-it-Yourself concept was compatible with carrying out the demands of Wright's designs. By serving as his own general contractor was Dad experiencing more problems than an experienced contractor would have done? Assuming Dad had been able to afford one, would he have been able to find a good contractor in the area who, in 1949, would have grasped the concept of Wright's design? Of course, we'll never have the answers to those questions, but it's interesting to speculate.

John Sergeant tells us,

"There were two methods of building used by Wright (before WW II): one utilized apprentice clerks-of-works and the other, master builders. The first involved the apprentice running the job by direct contracting, or acting as a general contractor. The second involved master builders Harold Turner and Ben Wiltscheck. These two men were retained by Wright on successive projects and learned to interpret his intentions almost by a sixth sense, and always with superb craftsmanship. When they handled a job they were never supervised. Their work with Taliesin only terminated with World War II, as did the contracting nature of apprentice superintendence. After 1945, there were usually general contractors appointed, while the apprentice superintended the project in a conventional way." [19]

In retrospect, Dad did a remarkable job of interpreting the plans and specifications for the house. Because of Wright's seeming nonchalance about providing many of the details, it couldn't have been easy. Dad had a real winner in Bob Cooper, who was intelligent, hard-working and a true problem-solver; and he had John Hill as his apprentice superintendent—in many ways the most valuable asset of all. Most importantly, he had Mother who, in spite of all the problems and frequent obstacles, was always there to back him up and pitch in wherever she was needed, and to keep our household running with little apparent effort. Difficult as it was at times, Mother and Dad were always able to keep the entire situation in perspective; they seemed quite able to maintain their sanity throughout, and roll with the punches whenever necessary. In fact, I think most of the time they really enjoyed it!

TWELVE

Visitors

As soon as construction had started and word got out that the Grants were building a Frank Lloyd Wright house, we began having visitors. Only a few came at first—the construction site was hard to find—but the number increased as the building progressed until, finally, there was an almost continuous stream of sightseers. They came for many reasons. Some were friends, neighbors and acquaintances, genuinely interested in following our progress; but sometimes the visitors were local people who came out of curiosity, often to scoff and dismiss the whole project as foolishness. At first, the workmen were self-conscious about having an audience. Before long, however, they began to enjoy it, and would have felt cheated if the visitors had stopped coming. It was the work crew who began telling us about some of the comments that were made by people viewing the construction for the first time. Many of the remarks were made by self-styled critics who were familiar with Wright's personal reputation only; others were strangers to his architecture and construction techniques and were puzzled, even irritated, by some of the things they saw at the site.

Supports for roof forms made from aspen trees. The source of much confusion.
Phil Feddersen

The supports for the roof forms were the source of at least one memorable comment. The specifications had called for a considerable number of very long, sturdy wood pilings to brace the weight of the roof until the concrete had set and the forms could be removed. Not only was Dad dismayed by what this lumber was going to cost, but he could see no use for it after it had served its purpose. Never a man to be defeated by a problem for very long, he came up with the idea of using Aspen tree trunks as supports. We had hundreds of these trees, they were easy to cut to size and put into place, and they could serve as firewood later. The idea worked perfectly but, visually, it was somewhat confusing. One afternoon, a group of visitors was completely bewildered by the small forest of Aspens that occupied the living room and most of the upper level. After studying the scene for a short time, one man finally said, with unconcealed contempt, "Well, I've heard that Frank Lloyd Wright sometimes leaves trees in his houses, but this is just ridiculous!"

Many visitors were teachers and students of architecture who admired Wright's work and were delighted by the opportunity to observe the construction of one of his houses at first hand. Frequently, these people came long distances to see the house, quite often from other countries. Mother and Dad began to realize, as they never had before, that they were doing something extraordinary. As work on the walls progressed, Wright began to mention the Grant house as an excellent example of using forms to lay a stone wall, always giving Dad credit for having devised this particular method. As a result, many came to look and ask questions about how it was done. These visitors almost always wrote or telephoned before they came, a courtesy we greatly appreciated, and we never refused a request to see the house from anyone who asked permission in advance. We kids became quite good at giving directions over the telephone, since Mother and Dad were usually at the building site. When strangers came to the door asking for either parent, they were directed to the site, which was the equivalent of two or three blocks away, by a casual wave of the hand in that general direction and a brief, "Down there."

One morning, while Mother was having an on-the-job lesson in spot welding, a group of visitors picked their way carefully through the tangle of electrical conduit and reinforcement steel to the spot where the work crew was gathered.

"Say," one of them called out, "We were told that Mrs. Grant was down here somewhere. Can you tell us where we might find her?"

With this, Mother flipped back her welder's mask and answered brightly, "I'm Mrs. Grant. What can I do for you?"

Mother loved these situations, and I know she was often deliberately slow to identify herself, prolonging the moment when she would have to reveal her cover and put an end to the candid remarks of her visitors. On a few occasions she preferred to remain incognito, particularly if the visitor was someone she wanted to avoid. These occasions never failed to convulse the work crew. The luckless soul who inquired in vain for

Mother and Bob Cooper at work on the living room fireplace.

Mrs. Grant must have thought we had a remarkably good-natured band of laborers, since they could be observed carrying out their various jobs to the accompaniment of great guffaws of laughter and badly concealed giggles.

One of those who toured the site without suspecting he was being monitored by my mother was an unnecessarily stuffy town dignitary of means who arrived one afternoon with his dowager mother, unannounced, to view the Frank Lloyd Wright house everyone was talking about. After walking around for a bit, dowager turned to son and said, "This house doesn't look very large; I thought Frank Lloyd Wright houses were bigger than this. There doesn't even seem to be a butler's pantry."

"Mother," he said, "these people probably don't have a butler."

"Really!" she exclaimed. "How do you suppose they manage without one?"

It's not difficult to imagine what the workmen were thinking while this conversation was taking place.

Many people were surprised by the concept of stone walls on the inside, as well as the outside. Some of the most frequently asked questions reflected that surprise. Upon being told that the walls inside would have nothing put on them in the way of an interior surface, there were comments such as:

"How will you hang wallpaper on your walls?"

"Will you paint the stone?"

One man asked Mother,

"How will you treat the stone?"

Having heard this question many times, Mother answered, somewhat snappishly, "We plan to treat it like stone."

The best visitors, and the ones we enjoyed the most, were the members of the Taliesin Fellowship who stopped to see us twice a year when they all drove from Wisconsin to Taliesin West in late fall and back again in the spring. They were always enthusiastic and appreciative of any progress made on the house, and they revived our sagging spirits when it seemed to us that we weren't moving very fast. There were many evenings when a few of them could be talked into staying for a home-cooked dinner, even spending the night. They all had sleeping bags and were used to spending the night wherever they were at the end of the day's driving. One year, they even had a refrigerated truck full of meat from the farm at Taliesin on its way to the desert camp in Scottsdale, which they plugged into an outdoor outlet for the night. Those evenings they spent with us were rare treats; the architectural students related stories about their life at Taliesin, and spoke of the excitement they felt at being able to study with Frank Lloyd Wright. Usually, someone had a guitar and could be coaxed into playing and singing. Their visits continued long after we moved into the house; these lively, talented people were always welcome.

The visitors we appreciated the most were the senior architects from the Taliesin staff who occasionally scheduled a trip to Cedar Rapids to visit the site. It was then that Dad could question what seemed to him to be inconsistencies in the working drawings, or simply get clarification on something he didn't understand. John Hill was particularly welcome, because there were always questions that couldn't be answered without seeing the problem at first hand. John almost always knew the answers and, if not, he could be counted on to get them quickly.

But the most important visitor had not been there yet.

Shortly after lunch, in early June 1950, Mother was catching up on household chores, something she rarely had time to do. It's a wonder she was home at all, since she was normally at the building site during the day, but there had been a thunderstorm that morning, accompanied by a major downpour, so the workmen had gone home and so had she. Mother enjoyed the work she did on the new house, but there were times when she found the work crew exasperating. Since they were still working mostly outside, a rain storm usually meant that they couldn't work until it was over. When the weather changed during the work day, and rain began to fall, they were quick to throw down their tools, exclaiming, "Oh, terrible rain storm! We can't work in this."

And off they would go. Never mind that the rain was only a passing shower and the sun came out an hour later; work was over for that day. Mother knew very well where they went when they left; there was a bar in nearby Marion, "The Scoreboard", where construction workers went when they were "at leisure". Mother always threatened to go down there and roust them out when the weather cleared, but of course she never did. The next day, however, she rarely failed to ask them, innocently, why they hadn't come back to work when fair weather returned.

By the end of a good, hard Iowa winter, the ground has usually frozen to a depth of about five feet. The ensuing spring thaw, which begins around the first of May, transforms the rich, fertile top soil and its underlying layer of clay into a gooey, sticky, bottomless mass of muck which is famous for its ability to pull rubber boots from the feet of small children and blasphemous oaths from the mouths of adult motorists. Exacerbated by the hard rain we'd just had, the building site that day was an excellent example of Iowa mud in its prime.

That afternoon, Mother received a telephone call from Gene Masselink, one of the senior architects at Taliesin who also served as Secretary to Mr. Wright.

> "Mrs. Grant, we're in Cedar Rapids and we'd like to come and visit the site, but we need directions on how to get there. Oh, and Mr. Wright is with us."

We all have different stories about who was where when the call came, but everyone remembers the haste with which toys and personal clutter were whisked out of sight, furniture dusted and cushions straightened. Mother's first act was to call Dad at the radio station. We owned only one automobile, so Dad had developed the practice of riding the bus into town to save gas rationing coupons during the war years. He walked to the bus line in the morning and back in the evening, using the car at night when he returned to the radio station to deliver the ten o'clock news broadcast. After the war ended, he often continued that routine; he enjoyed the walk, and the car was available if Mother needed it. As a result, our only car was home that day, and Mother would have to go and get Dad. After hurrying us into clean clothes, Mother tried to convey to us the magnitude of what was about to happen. We got the message loud and clear and we knew it was serious. Finally, she surveyed the scene, sighed, and said, "Well, at least Mr. Wright will understand why we need a new house!"

David and Linda went with Mother; David remembers a definite tension in the air on the way home. Mother and Dad were justifiably apprehensive about this visit, not so much because they would be entertaining Frank Lloyd Wright in their home for the first time, although that was certainly a factor. It was mostly because he had not yet seen the construction and the stonework. What if he didn't like the stone when he finally saw it in the walls, or what if he thought they were bungling the job?

I had been left at home to finish the clean-up and to be there if the Wright party arrived before Mother and Dad did. To my great relief, Mother and Dad arrived at about the same time that a small caravan of Cherokee Red cars pulled up in front of the house. I don't recall who was in all of those cars, certainly Gene Masselink and John Hill were, but there was no mistaking the stately figure emerging from one of them, resplendent in suit and tie, cape and pork pie hat. Frank Lloyd Wright had come to call!

Mother liked to plan events well in advance whenever possible, but Wright was not one to worry about convenience; I've since learned that his visits to clients were more often than not completely unannounced. Considering the situation, Mother handled things very well, I thought. While Dad joined Wright and the architects at the site, she busied herself preparing refreshment for the group and, when they returned, we were all treated to iced tea and homemade cookies. The afternoon went well. Wright was pleased with the way the house was progressing and generous with compliments about the way the masons were laying the stone. Too bad they weren't there to hear it from the source. He said he was particularly impressed with the "fabric" of the walls, an unusual description of stonework that we had never heard before. I'd be willing to bet that Mother was more than a little disappointed that she didn't have the opportunity to join the group for the walk around the building site. She had put a lot of time and hard work into this project, and it would have been gratifying to hear Wright's comments at first hand.

However, Mother and Dad were overjoyed now that the Official Blessing had been bestowed. Everyone gathered on the screened porch of the little brown house, with Wright presiding graciously over the assembled group, seemingly oblivious to the mud that clung to his elegant shoes and pant legs. He had thoughtfully suggested that we lay a path of newspapers across the living room floor to protect Mother's carpet from the mud on his shoes, which we hastened to do. Unsurprisingly, no one requested that he remove his shoes!

I am still impressed when I recall how he seemed to genuinely enjoy the occasion. He had a remarkable ability to make others feel at ease if he wanted to, and he quite clearly approved of my parents. He hadn't been there long before he had us talking freely about our hobbies and what we were learning at school. The adults talked about the house and other things that occupy the attention of adults. Mother relaxed to the point where, to my complete horror, she insisted upon trotting out my latest efforts at drawing and painting. Helpful criticism and encouragement were generously and honestly given, as only a true gentleman and diplomat would do under the circumstances. Wright remembered that Mother had been wearing her hair long the last time he saw her. She replied that she had cut it short so it wouldn't get in her eyes when she worked in the quarry. It's probably safe to say that he had never heard that explanation for a hair-style from any other woman. He clearly found her reply remarkable, because he quoted it when he talked to the Fellowship about the Grant house upon his return to Taliesin.

But soon he had to leave and, despite the fact that we had been thrown into turmoil by his visit, we were genuinely sorry to see him go. As we all accompanied him to his car, Wright turned and regarded my brother, David. Now nine years old, David had developed a habit of standing with his thumbs hooked in the front pockets of his jeans, as he was doing at that moment. Wright said to him,

"Young man, if you continue to stand that way you will grow up with terrible posture. Do you see how it makes your shoulders hunch forward? If you must put your hands in your pockets, then put them in your back pockets. That throws the shoulders back, you see, and makes you stand straighter."

David accepted the advice with his usual good nature and vowed that he would change his ways. As the last red car pulled away from the house to a chorus of goodbyes, we felt as if a whirlwind had come and gone. I'm sure Mother and Dad had much to talk about that night; it had been a highly important occasion for them and one that none of us would ever forget. And, from that day on, whenever David put his hands in his front pockets, Mother never lost the opportunity to say,

"Remember what Mr. Wright told you."

But it never did any good. He still stands that way.

The consensus in the Grant household was that the long-awaited visit from Mr. Wright had been a success, in spite of mud. I wish I knew more about what they talked about while they walked around the building site, but apparently it went quite well. It was only after everyone had gone that Dad realized he had been so preoccupied with Wright's visit to the site, and subsequent judgment of the progress being made, that he had forgotten to take any photographs of the momentous event. It was an omission we have always regretted, because it was the only visit from Frank Lloyd Wright we ever had.

Two days later, Wright addressed the Taliesin Fellowship as usual at Sunday morning breakfast. This is, in part, what he said:

"We have just come back from a trip to (a building that has) been going on all winter.

"We were worried—I was—about the Grant house, because he was with his wife in a stone quarry getting out the stones to build his house with, didn't have too much money but was building about a $50,000 house, and sent photographs of it (a sample wall), and neglected to put a human being in to get the scale. So I took the scale to be about like this wall, here. And I was alarmed, and then when I saw it the stones were about the thickness of your hand, about as long as two hands, or one hand, sometimes as thick as two hands; and he had produced a remarkably beautiful texture. With stone—no mortar—it was his idea; he put up the forms on either side, of wood; then he had a little iron bracing in case…So he has really invented something. And he got the stone out of the quarry himself—he didn't ask any help, he and his wife. She shook her head with all her little short curls; she'd cut her hair off so it wouldn't get in her eyes when working.

"So this is an American proceeding—building their own house. And they certainly ought to have a house—they're all tumbled up in a pile with three children, and the parents, but they're getting a lot of fun out of that house, I know. It is going to be beautiful—a new thing in the way of masonry has come to town, you see, because there is no trowel on the face of that thing at all, there is no mortar even; you can stick your hand in about that far all along the outside crevices in that wall. And the color is beautiful, of that stone. In the quarry it flakes; a kind of limestone deposit that comes out in little flakes like crackers. So he's going to have a beautiful house, and it's about…the chimney's finished, and the second story is poured, and he's now busy bending the conduit and putting it in the walls and floors himself.

"He's no electrician; never had done anything of that kind before. He's a radio man, a very bright fellow. If every G.I. had the wit and intelligence to go ahead and build a house the way he's building his, our colleges would be greatly relieved. Yes, pleasing, astonishing, to see what he does." [20]

It was several years before Mother and Dad learned of that glowing tribute paid to them by Wright. I often wonder, had they known about it at the time, how they would have reacted. I'm sure it would have given their spirits a lift to carry them through the roughest of spots. I don't believe Wright lavished praise on his clients very often—at least to that degree.

THIRTEEN

The House Takes Shape

Shortly before the Wright visit took place, Dad had written to John Hill with a progress report which, in retrospect, may very well have contributed to Wright's decision to go see the house.

"Many thanks for clearing up the matter of the stairway wall and the misplaced footings. I forgot to answer your question about the stone for copings. I think we have located some at Stone City which will match the rest of the wall in color. It's somewhat softer, but probably will last several thousand years. Hope you received the photos all right and that the walls bear a reasonable resemblance to what you and Mr. Wright had in mind. We have done no pointing-up whatever, so far; preferring to wait until you or Mr. Wright can actually see the walls, then make specific recommendations. Outside of a few minor flaws which are correctable, Mrs. Grant and I are pleased.

"I have now quite given up on the steel casements. Please proceed with the details for cypress. One detail I'd like to have by return mail if possible. Can you tell me the thickness of the stock you will use, so my local mill-work supplier can be sure to have it on hand. They're placing an order for a car-load of cypress in the next few days and they'd like to include this in the order.

"I am enclosing a color chart of the concrete floor color material handled by my regular masonry supplier. Will you please let me know if this particular brand is okay and, if so, which shade we should employ. With reasonable luck on the weather, we should be ready to pour the upper floor slab before the end of April."

In May, they built the forms for the upstairs floors and the balcony floors and walls which were all to be of concrete and, when that was done, they poured the concrete for the entire second floor. The concrete for the floors was poured into forms with screeds, or thickness guides, used to insure that the concrete would be poured to the right level. The height from floor to ceiling was specified at 6'9", so the thickness of the poured floor was crucial. While the concrete was still wet, powdered Colorundum pigment was applied to the wet surface and painstakingly smoothed until it was distributed evenly. The color used in the Grant house was of course Wright's favorite, Cherokee Red. The finisher employed to perform this important task was an Italian artisan, named Giacomo, who was hired from the union hall and said to be "the best in the business". However, Bob Cooper was not pleased with the work Giacomo did, particularly when he found out that "the best in the business" had pulled the screeds out so he would be able to reach into the corners more easily. This meant that some areas of the floor on the upper level were now slightly higher than they should be, at least until Bob Cooper discovered what was happening. Giacomo spoke and read only Italian; he couldn't read the directions on the Colorundum package, so he guessed at what they said. Before long, it was clear that this was not going to be a satisfactory working relationship, and no one was surprised that Giacomo was no longer part of the work force when the time came to pour the lower level floors. Bob Cooper decided he would rather do the job himself. Somehow, in spite of all these drawbacks, the floors turned out quite

Stone work in the master bedroom. South balcony is at left, fireplace and east wall at right. Phil Feddersen

well. The kitchen floor was the only exception; apparently there was too much water in that particular batch of concrete. As a result, the texture was too rough and the surface did not take the color well. At the time it was not so apparent, but in later years the surface did not hold up as well to normal wear. That is the only place where it happened, however.

That summer, stone was laid for the upstairs walls to roof level, and the stone pier was built in the car port. When I was a child, my friends and I devised many ingenious ways of amusing ourselves outdoors. One favorite was to rake autumn leaves into floor plans of "houses" composed of one-dimensional rooms that had doors, windows and corridors where we would play happily for hours, acting out stories we made up about life in our houses. As soon as we had floors in our new house, we suddenly had a real-life version of that game. Now we could walk through these spaces, trying to imagine what life would be like, once we really lived here. But it was still a major challenge to the imagination to do so.

In September 1950 they poured the concrete floors for the dining room, kitchen and utility areas. After the color was applied, but while the concrete was still wet, snap-lines were attached to forms at four foot square intervals, which resulted in lines incised in the floor to emphasize the four foot units on which the design for the house was based. Once the floors had set up, the furnace was installed. Things were beginning to happen much more quickly now.

I haven't yet described the house as it would appear to someone seeing it for the first time. Up to this point I wanted to concentrate on all the steps leading to its inception and the slow, but steady, progress of the construction. But now that the house has the beginnings of floors, walls and ceilings, I'll jump ahead and take you on a tour of the house. My hope is that you will be better able to visualize what I'm talking about when I continue the story.

You drive down a long, gently curving driveway at the east end of the house. Only a small part of the house is visible from here: one end of the cantilevered concrete slab roof which appears to rest on a large stone pier, the car port, and the east end of the master bedroom and locker room; there are no windows on this side, except for a corner window in the master sitting room which is obscured on this side by shrubbery. You walk down a flagstone walk on the north side of the house, under the roof overhang, which ends in a stone wall. To the left of the wall is the main entrance to the house. As you walk toward it, you get your first view of the spectacular view to the north and west, as the terrain drops off sharply on both sides. The landscape is one of rolling green hills, ending in a wooded area below, broken only by trees ranging from flowering fruit trees to stately maples.

The double glass entrance doors lead to a flagstone loggia, or entrance hall, with built-in benches for informal seating. As you enter and look to your right, you find yourself standing at the top of one of the most remarkable stairways to be found in any of the houses that Wright designed. In his book, *Taliesin Drawings,* Edgar Kaufmann, Jr. describes it this way:

> "To the right marches one of the most grand and dramatic stairways ever invented, straight as an arrow between two steeply rising walls of stone, for over forty feet. On the right the wall is crowned with a shallow glass strip, and, just as it begins at a glass doorway, so it ends with a tall glass vertical which separates it from a brief stub of stone set at right angles and terminating the onward sweep of the stairwell. The left wall of the stairwell is in part a low parapet guarding the bedroom hall from the incline of steps. Beyond this, the chimney mass rises to the roof. So much can be seen as one enters, and a high screen of glass at the far end of the living room." [21]

To the left of the main entrance is a door to the locker room, a place for changing out of work clothes and muddy play clothes, with a small bathroom, wooden lockers for clothes and shelves for storage. There is also a stairway down to the lower level utility area. Past the locker room on the left side of the loggia is a small corridor to the master bedroom suite. Typical of many Wright houses, the corridor seems narrow and cramped for a bit until you emerge into the bright, sunny room that was my parents' haven for so many years. The room faces south and the entire south wall is glass, with casement doors leading onto a small terrace. There is a large fireplace in one corner of the room and a full bath on the north side. The only windows in the bathroom, as well as the locker room, are small rectangular slots reminiscent of gun emplacements in a bunker. The workmen, many of whom were war veterans, liked to joke that it would be a good place to "pick off the enemy as they came across the valley", but as far as I know, none ever appeared. All furniture in this room is built in, with the exception of the bed. There is ample wardrobe space all

Walkway to the main entrance, View of the valley below.

Entrance loggia, door to south balcony.

along one wall and several built-in bookshelves. Returning to the loggia, you next encounter a coat closet at the far left. Opposite the entrance doors are similar doors leading out to the balcony that starts here and runs down the entire south side of the upper level.

Also on the upper level, and to the far right of the entrance, is the corridor that leads to the children's bathroom and bedrooms. First is the bathroom, which is so small that it's a wonder they were able to fit in a toilet, lavatory, shower stall and linen closet. As it was, Dad had to look a long time for a shower stall that would fit into the space allotted to it. It is impossible for two people to be in that bathroom at the same time. An adult with a reasonably slim build can shower, but it isn't very comfort-

West view of balcony, doors to children's bedrooms.

able and, when it's time to towel off, there is only a two feet square area in which to do so. The only air supply is a door leading onto the balcony. It is not a bathroom that encourages lingering.

The next two rooms along the corridor were David's and Linda's bedrooms. They are mirror images of each other and nearly identical in size. Furniture consists of a single, built-in bed in one corner, with a desk and chair next to it. Above the desk and bed are built-in book shelves, which can be a definite safety hazard at times. Anyone who sleeps there learns quickly not to sit up in bed suddenly; the result is a painful bump on the head. The wall opposite the bed contains a built-in wardrobe with an accordion door. One begins to understand, after seeing these rooms, that Wright considered bathrooms and bedrooms to be purely utilitarian. The family is meant to gather and socialize in the main living spaces of the home. At the end of the corridor is the remaining bedroom, which was mine while I was still living at home. It is considerably larger than the other two and looks down into the two-story living room from a casement window. There is, despite Mr. Wright's promise to me, no fireplace in this room; there wouldn't have been room for both a fireplace and a bed. There was no favoritism intended in Wright's assignment of rooms; the decision was simply based on common sense. The eldest child would probably be the first to leave home, thereby freeing up the room for guests. All of the bedrooms have window walls to the south and access to the balcony.

At the foot of the staircase, which is lined with bookshelves on the right wall and lighted by recessed lights above and clerestory windows high up near the ceiling, you emerge from the long, dark passage of the stairway into the large, brightly-lighted open space that is the two-story living room. The effect is stunning, and is meant to be. Until now, you have seen mostly small, utilitarian living spaces. Suddenly you are confronted with a space that almost overwhelms you with its magnitude. Recently I returned from a trip to some of the medieval walled towns

View from loggia down the main stairway.

Looking up the stairway from the living room.

off the coasts of Montenegro and Croatia. Walking down some of those narrow, dark streets to arrive unexpectedly at an open, spacious square, I was reminded of the passage down the stairway into the Grant living room. Three sides of the room are glass window walls, with panoramic views of the surrounding countryside that change with the seasons. In winter there is a blanket of white broken only by the bare bones of trees. Spring brings the trees to life as the countryside turns green. Summer's hot sun is partially blocked by the wide overhang of the roof, and the cool stone walls of the house are a welcome refuge from the heat. Fall is particularly beautiful when the big old maple tree outside the corner of the living room turns spectacular shades of yellow, orange and red. There can be no lovelier way to decorate a room than the ever-changing color and light that nature provides.

There is a fireplace in one corner in which an adult could stand upright. None of the fireplaces in the house have mantels or formal, raised hearths; the flagstone base is flush with the stone or concrete floors. There are no andirons; logs are stood on end against the back of the fire chamber or fed into it from the front, depending on the length of the logs. When we were living there, the living room fireplace gave an entirely new dimension to our Sunday evening fires; a cozy fire was more like a roaring inferno when it was really stoked up.

Three steps up from the flagstone floor of the living room and you are in the dining room, with another, smaller fireplace. This room has space for a sound system and record storage built into the south wall, which continues around the corner into the kitchen. There is a built-in banquette on the wall between the kitchen and dining room, affording seating for the dining table. An accordion door leads out to a landing on the grand staircase just before the final steps to the living room; on that landing is a recessed wood storage closet within easy reach of both downstairs fireplaces. Beyond the dining room is, of course, the kitchen. Mother had made it clear to Wright that she wanted a good-sized and well-lighted kitchen because she spent so much time there. For her, the kitchen was not just another utilitarian space meant to function only as the service area for the dining room. Mother loved to cook and she considered the kitchen her studio; it needed to be a pleasant place in which to work. The view outside the kitchen windows was a particularly fine one, and Mother wanted to be able to enjoy it as she went about her work. She pretty much got what she asked for. Instead of the high clerestory windows that Wright typically employed in his clients' kitchens, we had a combination of casement and fixed-glass windows that provided a generous view of the lawn and garden on the south side of the house and a source of cool breezes to dispel any heat or unwelcome odors produced by the cooking process.

The utility room is beyond the kitchen and, from this point on, you are under ground. The area next to the kitchen houses the furnace and water heater and a small area for Dad's tools. Next is a large storage space for preserved food and overflow kitchen storage, followed by the laundry area and Dad's photographic darkroom, which is under the back stairway to the locker room. A chest model freezer sits in an alcove next to a door to the outside; when you emerge from this exit you are below, and to the left of the main entrance on the upper level. As kids, we used to tell friends that our back door and our front door were right next to each other.

FOURTEEN

A Concrete Slab Roof

Picnics were a favorite activity at Taliesin. Whenever the weather was fine, Wright suggested that luncheon be moved outdoors to one of several grassy areas on the grounds. Blankets were spread on the grass for the Fellowship and Taliesin guests, and the apprentices served appropriate picnic fare to all assembled. Mother and Dad attended several of these gatherings and, during one of them, were treated to a typical Wright witticism: as everyone was finding a spot to sit, campstools were brought out for Mr. and Mrs. Wright. As Wright sat down on his stool, it began to tip on the uneven ground and it appeared that the Great Man would be unceremoniously dumped onto the ground. As the people near him rushed to prevent him from falling, he laughed and assured them that he was fine, saying, "I've been fighting gravity all my life".

The concept of a cantilevered, 127 foot long, poured concrete slab roof was hard for many people to understand in 1949; maybe it still is. When Dad went to the Guaranty Bank and Trust Co. in Cedar Rapids to discuss partial financing for building the house, the working drawings were greeted with some skepticism. Dad was well known to everyone at the bank, and it was no surprise to anyone there that he was planning to build a Frank Lloyd Wright house. However, there was at least one member of the loan committee who had grave doubts about the project and those doubts were mostly centered on the cantilevered roof. By agreeing to help finance the building of this house, the bank could be backing a project that might never succeed. Some believed it would be just a matter of time before the whole thing came crashing down. Apparently, by 1939, several of Wright's clients who depended on loans from the Federal Housing Authority were refused financing because of the Usonian house's unconventional design. They were, therefore, forced to rely on either local financing or the family nest-egg, or to give up the project altogether. [22]

It couldn't have been easy for Dad to ask for that loan. He had been raised, as had most of his generation, to believe that you pay as you go along; if you don't have enough money to buy something, you do without it. However, he and Mother had borrowed to build their first house and again when they bought the additional land from the county. Dad was wise enough to understand that extraordinary circumstances call for extraordinary measures. The opportunity to build a Wright house would probably never come their way again. Dad raised a large part of the building cost by selling some of the original fifty acres of the land they owned; nevertheless, additional funding was a vital element of the construction budget. Fortunately, the more foresighted officers at the bank prevailed and agreed to the loan, providing building costs could be kept at a reasonable level—as if that wasn't Dad's objective already. In later years, the president of the bank told Dad, "If I'd known what a great house it would turn out to be, I'd have encouraged you to default on the loan!"

In the fall of 1950 the forms for the roof were constructed, using the aforementioned Aspen tree trunks for support. Wandering around the interior, amid all those trees, was a remarkable experience. It's no won-der that many visitors to the house at the time were completely taken aback by the sight of what appeared to be a small forest within the house. It's also understandable that many were confused, registering an entire range of reactions from disbelief to contempt, by what they saw. The entire concept of Wright's design philosophy was completely new to most people in Cedar Rapids. The prevalent view of what should consti-tute one's dream house was still based on traditional architecture. Many had never heard of Wright at all; they were there because they were curi-ous. Most people who came to see what was going on had no idea what to expect, and the trees no doubt reinforced their belief that this was sheer craziness. Wright would have loved it!

At its lowest point, over the carport end of the house, the roof would be about seven feet from the ground. It was at that end that a wide wooden ramp was built, providing access to the huge wooden forms into which concrete would be poured for the roof slab. The workmen called it the "Pyramid Ramp"; we kids ran up and down it every chance we got. Since the roof would also serve as the ceiling for the upper level and the living room, it would have to be smooth on the underside; therefore, the big, flat "floor" of the forms was lined with Masonite, smooth side up. At this point it was also necessary to install all of the electrical conduit and the wooden light box molds that Dad had devised into what would become the ceiling. Mother and Dad greased the light box molds with axle grease so they would come loose once the concrete had set up. The roof forms were fitted around the steel mullions that projected from the living room window-walls and from the tops of all the outside stone walls, and a layer of 4' x 8' Steelcrete mesh was welded to the mullion tops. Steel reinforce-ment rods were placed inside the facia at the outer edge of the roof, and a second layer of mesh was put down. Now, with both layers of steel mesh in place, it only remained to install the chimney flues and the vent pipes.

By October the trees had turned and the leaves were beginning to fall.

West end of living room, supports for roof forms. Phil Feddersen

I thought the big Maple at the corner of the living room was unusually beautiful that fall. Maybe that was because, by walking up the ramp to the roof form, I could settle down in a spot that was almost up in the tree's branches. With all that bright color around me, a spectacular view of the entire valley below and the warm fall sun making it quite comfortable, I had found an ideal spot to do my school homework. Geometry was a lot more fun to do up on the roof! It was such a pleasant place to be on nice days that we almost hated to spoil it by pouring the concrete.

But on Monday October 16 they began pouring the roof. It was a tremendous job that commanded the attention, concentration and stamina of everyone involved, because no one on this job had ever done anything like this before. Bob Cooper had decided not to use a crane and bucket to pour the concrete because he didn't want to run the risk of putting undue strain on the form support system; the crane method might result

South view of the house with roof forms nearly completed.

in too much concrete being dumped in one place all at once. Therefore, the concrete was poured into wheelbarrows, wheeled up the ramp by a small army comprised of every farmer Bob Cooper could round up, as well as workmen and volunteer friends, who dumped it into the form. The leaves, which looked so lovely floating down from the trees, were also floating into the steel mesh. As luck would have it, a strong wind blew all through the night before the pour and, by morning, the big Maple tree had lost all of its leaves—a large number sticking in the crevices of the mesh. It was Mother's job to precede the barrows of concrete coming up the ramp and get rid of the leaves and twigs that were lodged there. She tried sweeping them off, but most leaves were stuck deep in the mesh. The openings were small and reaching down into them was difficult, as the mesh was almost an inch thick and two layers deep in places. The steel edges were sharp, but gloves were out of the question because wearing them prevented her from picking up the leaves. She soon had

Pouring the concrete roof. Dad is on left holding up the steel mesh.

so many small lacerations on her hands that they were bleeding steadily; however, no one thought that blood in the concrete was anywhere near as bad as leaves would have been!

They took a big chance working with that much concrete so late in the season. Rain could be a problem, but worse still would be an early freeze that might prevent the concrete from setting up properly, thereby ruining the entire job. At this point, however, they had to risk it. The building schedule had been drawn up with little margin for delay, and it was mandatory that the roof be completed before winter set in so that work could go on inside when the weather turned cold. They were running out of time.

There were some problems, but not major ones. They used sixty-four cubic yards of concrete in the roof, delivered by trucks that held three cubic yards each. Unfortunately, one concrete supplier ran through his inventory before the job was finished, requiring Dad and Bob Cooper to hastily round up the remainder from another company. On the first day they poured the concrete from the west end of the roof to a point above the children's bathroom. During the pouring process, one person ran a vibration probe to make sure there were no air spaces or holes in the concrete. Dad's job was to ensure that the steel mesh remained at the correct height by walking ahead of the wheelbarrows and lifting it up to keep it level as the concrete was dumped on top. It was also important to keep the mesh from resting on the form below because, if that happened, the mesh might show through the ceiling of the upper level. Dad was also responsible for seeing to it that no concrete got into the recessed light boxes and their conduits.

Some time before all this took place, Mother had worried that concrete "juice" would run down the cracks in the places where the roof met the stone surfaces of the inside walls when the concrete was poured. She had the idea that, by stuffing folded-up pieces of newspaper into all the cracks, this could be prevented. She was partially right. The job of wedging all that newspaper into all the cracks was nowhere near as tedious as it was to dig them out again, once they had become encrusted with hardened concrete. I'd be willing to bet you could still find some of them up there if you looked hard enough.

Many people came to watch the job, some out of curiosity and some to help. The first evening, after everyone had gone home for the day, there was another visitor to the site. When Bob Cooper arrived the next morning he discovered, to his disgust, that a very large dog had walked through the wet concrete the night before. All of the activity surrounding the pouring of the roof took place without any of the Grant children there to enjoy it; any suggestion of skipping school to watch was met with total resistance. I am reasonably sure that, as much as they loved us, Mother and Dad were relieved to have us comfortably out of the way for the time it took to pour the roof. And it took only two days, because their luck held, the weather remained fair, nothing else went wrong and they poured the east end of the roof from the loggia to the carport the next day.

A mixture of vermiculite and concrete was poured on top of the slab, oce it set up. This was a relatively new product, called "Zonelite", and it was meant to provide insulation. Now, the stonemasons were able to finish building the two big chimneys by laying stone around the flues where they rose above the roof. While that was taking place, laminated panels made of tar and roofing felt were applied as a water barrier, in accord with Wright's specifications. However, when Wright specified those laminated felt panels, he neglected to explain how they were to be fastened down. Bob Cooper worked out a method for doing so, but it was not totally satisfactory; there was always a worry that they would come up in a big wind storm. It wasn't until many years later that Dad finally figured out how to secure them successfully.

Why did Wright design a flat roof for a house in Iowa, and why did Dad agree to it? In *The Natural House*, Wright says,

"On the other hand, snow is the best kind of insulation. You do not have to buy it. In northern climates you can see how well a house is insulated by noticing how quickly the snow melts off the roof. If the snow stays for some time, the roof is pretty well insulated. If you get insulation up to a certain point, snow will come and give you more. To hold snow on the roof is always a good, wise provision and a good argument for a flat roof" [23]

The roof was designed to withstand a much heavier load than any snow that would accumulate during the winter; that wasn't a worry. But what would happen in spring when the snow began to melt and the copious spring rains arrived? There was a drainage system for the roof and the latest waterproofing techniques were used. Dad was assured by Wright, as well as everyone he consulted in the roofing business, that the roof would be water tight.

When I talked to Edgar Kaufmann, Jr. in 1979, I asked him if the roofs at "Fallingwater" had ever leaked. He joked, with a hearty laugh, "Of course they leaked! All of Mr. Wright's flat roofs leak!"

True or not, the Grant house certainly did; it leaked from the beginning of the first spring. Expansion and contraction are to be expected in a concrete slab roof. The process, although quite normal, can sometimes be a bit unnerving, though. Waking abruptly in the middle of a sub-zero winter night to what sounds like very loud gun shots is not conducive to restful sleep, even if you know what it is. However, some of those contractions were bound to result in hairline (and some not so hairline) cracks in the concrete, and Dad worried that the water collecting on the roof would find its way through all that waterproofing and come, via the cracks, dripping down into our house.

The workmen waited three or four weeks for the concrete to set up, not wanting to take any chances by removing the supports too soon. The day the forms were to come off, Dad had pressing business at the radio station, so the task fell to Bob Cooper and his crew, with Mother as an apprehensive spectator. Apparently, the workmen were a little more nervous about the job than they had let on, because they knocked out the key supports one at a time, stepping well back from the roof each time they did so. When they were finally convinced that the massive slab was going to stay up there, they reacted with a spontaneous round of applause. Then they set about removing the forms and the Pyramid Ramp with great enthusiasm, anxious now to see what the roof would look like in all its unencumbered splendor.

Visually, it is a splendid roof. It begins gently, almost as part of the hillside, appearing to rest lightly on the stone pier of the carport. Then it soars out into space, seeming to float above the expanse of glass that is the living room, far above the landscape below. But, before one is tempted to call it an intrusion on that landscape, the eye returns to the glorious old Maple outside the southwest corner of the living room, which arches above the roof, connecting the house to the land. You then see the stone retaining wall of the south terrace which begins at the base of the living room and curves gently around until it disappears into the slope, returning the house to the hillside from which it comes. Leaky or not, there could be no other roof for that house.

FIFTEEN

What Will It Be Like to Live Here?

When it began to look as if the house would be finished enough for us to move into before the year was over, Mother and Dad put the little brown house up for sale. It was soon purchased by good friends, both teachers at one of the local high schools. We were pleased that they would be our neighbors and even more pleased that the first house Mother and Dad built, where we spent many happy years, would now belong to someone who genuinely loved it. When January 1, 1951 was agreed upon as a closing date, it seemed a long way off; however, it was now the winter of 1950, and our new house was far from finished.

During that winter, plate glass was installed between the steel mullions, which had been painted the same dark red as the floors, and glass was placed in all exterior doors. The large plate glass panels for the living room had not been shipped because there was a strike at the plant where they were being made, halting production for a considerable period of time. The glass for the clerestory panes above the stairway had been shipped earlier, but turned out to be the wrong size. Since faulty measurement was the company's error, they were replaced at no extra cost.

The panels had, of course, been cut to order and were useless to the glass company, so they were stacked in an out-of-the-way corner for a time, but they were not forgotten. They eventually became windows in the workshop that Dad and David built several years later. Dad never liked to waste good building material!

Wright did not specify thermal (or insulated double glass) panels for his houses. He believed that Gravity Heating made thermal panes unnecessary and was fond of saying, "You won't need it; it would be like a dog with two tails."

It wasn't until several years later, when heating the vast, two-story space of the living room became a real problem, that John Hill told Dad he could use thermal glass if he wanted to. But, even if Wright had allowed it at the time, thermal windows were still a relatively new concept and would have been prohibitively expensive.

Hanging the big exterior doors of the living room presented logistic problems. Wright had specified brass piano hinges for all of the high, narrow, glass-paneled cypress doors, which was a stroke of genius. Ordinary door hinges would never have stood the strain placed on them by the sheer weight of each door. He neglected, however, to specify how the hinges were to be attached to the steel mullions. Mother and Dad finally solved this problem by welding one side of the hinge directly to the steel, which worked very well; however, it meant that the other side of the hinge had to be attached to the door while holding it in place. I don't think it was necessary to actually put a screw through every one of the holes in the piano hinges; that would have taken months. Every third or fourth hole seems to have been enough; the hinges are still performing quite well after all these years.

All of the concrete floors had been poured and finished, but we didn't have any flagstone floors yet. Dad and Bob Cooper had always known that the rock from our quarry would not be suitable for flagstone floors because it flaked too easily and could not be cut thick enough for flagstones. For similar reasons, it couldn't be used for the front stairs; they would require big, thick slabs of stone. The previous summer, Dad learned that the city of Cedar Rapids was about to begin a major renovation of the streets around the central town square. This would involve widening most of the present streets and tearing out the original limestone curbs that had been there since about 1850. A neighbor who was working for the contractor on the project approached Dad and asked him if we could use any additional stone for the house. He said they were going to haul it to the dump and, if he was interested, Dad could have it for the price of trucking it away. Dad became extremely interested as soon as he went to inspect the stone. Unlike the six inch curbs of today, these curbs were made of large slabs of limestone and were big, thick and too high for modern car doors. But for our purposes they were perfect, since they were of uniform size and color. So Dad acquired all the stone he needed—56 tons in all—for $102.41! Everyone was happy with the deal, and we now had the material for our flagstone floors and grand stairway.

It was becoming clear that the winter of 1950-1951 was going to be an unusually harsh one. Stone often becomes too brittle to work with in freezing weather, and Bob Cooper thought it was too cold to risk trying to chip the stone to size. That meant the entrance loggia floor and the stone stairway to the living room would have to wait until warmer weather in the spring. Dad had known for some time that he wouldn't be able to lay the stone for the living room floor and the two stone terraces until after we had moved into the house, partly because the living room would not be closed in during the winter, but also because he didn't have enough time. Now we would just have to manage with only the back stairway from the locker room to the utility area as our means of getting from one level to the other, at least until summer. Of course, the back stairway hadn't been built yet, either! Fortunately, that work could be done inside where it was reasonably warm, thanks to the new furnace.

First, however, the chest freezer had to be lowered down the hole where the back stairway would eventually be. Construction of the back stairs actually took very little time and, with its completion, we were another step closer to moving date.

Since a large part of the living room was without glass and had no floor, and the stone stairway was nothing but a dirt ramp, neither area would be part of the living space into which we were about to move. Therefore, plywood was placed in the empty spaces where glass was missing, and the living room was boarded off from the dining room and the bottom of the stairway. A large brown canvas tarpaulin was rigged up at the top of the stairway in an attempt to keep drafts from below from invading the upstairs. There were no partitions between the children's bedrooms and no doors on the bathrooms. The main entrance door could not be used, because there was only a rudimentary concrete sub-floor in the loggia. Dad laid plywood across the rough concrete so we could walk across it to our bedrooms, but the only entrance to the house was through the lower grade door to the utility area.

The movers had been scheduled to arrive on Thursday, December 28, but that morning we learned that the van had stalled in a snowstorm in Chicago and wouldn't arrive until the following day. All of our belongings were packed and ready to go, but we had dinner that night at the home of friends, then returned home for an early bed time. The movers arrived at 8:15 the next morning. So, with no ceremony to mark the occasion, we left the cramped, but warm and cozy, little brown house we had lived in for so long, and moved into our Frank Lloyd Wright house.

It was bitterly cold that day, but we were all so busy with the move we didn't have time to think about it. There wasn't a lot of furniture to be moved, but decisions had to be made about where to put it when it arrived at the new house. The furniture from Mother and Dad's bedroom went into the master suite, whether it was suitable or not. David and Linda had built-in beds in their new rooms, but the bed I was currently using was moved into my new room. We had no closets yet, so bureaus were pressed into service for the present. There wasn't room for much else in the bedrooms. I seem to remember that the living room sofa spent the winter in the space that would someday become the front stairway, and the dining room table—one of the first pieces of furniture that Mother and Dad bought when they married—went into the new dining room, where it looked small and out of place. Of course there were boxes and crates everywhere, stacked along walls and corridors. Knowing how practical Mother was, I'm sure they were well labeled and had been placed in more-or-less the area where they would be needed. The cartons of books, alone, took up a great deal of space. The built-in bookshelves that were to run the length of the stairwell were not considered a high-priority item just yet, so the books would remain in their cartons for an indefinite period. At noon, we took a welcome break for lunch at a nearby friend's house, but soon returned to plunge into the frenzy again.

I'd like to believe that David, Linda and I were a big help during the move; we were out of school for Christmas recess. Mother said we helped carry things into the house, but we mostly stayed out of the way; we had the master bedroom fireplace and the warm floors to make us comfortable. David and Linda had fun reading the old newspapers that had been used as packing material, and David found Dad's old typewriter, which mysteriously typed letters that were black on top and red on the bottom, and amused himself by typing for a while. Eventually we escaped to the locker room, to draw pictures and read. As it began to get dark, we found something we could do. The partitions separating the three children's bedrooms had not yet been built, so there was a high degree of urgency to rig up bureaus, blankets and sheets for privacy. This was accomplished, but not without a lot of giggling and teasing.

When everything had been moved into the house and put somewhere—or just anywhere there was room, Mother and Dad were exhausted. Several weeks before the move, a great many of our friends, guessing at the toll this move would take on my parents, had thoughtfully offered to feed us dinner the night of the move; but, since the move was a day late, the subsequent confusion resulted in no dinner invitation at all. When the time for dinner was rapidly approaching, Mother suddenly realized that she had a hungry family to feed. The electric stove had not yet been hooked up, and she had no idea of where in all those boxes there might be something she could give us for dinner. Even if they had mustered the strength to go and get it, this was long before the era of take-out food. As if there weren't already enough problems, the water in the well pit had frozen the night before, which meant we had no running water. Our first meal in the new house was hotdogs, cooked over the fire in the master bedroom fireplace, speared on our camping forks. It was delicious! Soon after, we kids gratefully fell into beds made up with sheets, blankets and pillows that Mother had, somehow, known where to find in all those boxes.

After we went to bed, Dad uncrated and hooked up the new electric stove. Neighbors arrived with a big pot of hot coffee and the adults sat around the fire in the master bedroom talking, until everyone could see that Mother and Dad were ready to drop from exhaustion. At last they were able to go to bed; they were tired, but relieved that the move had finally been accomplished, despite a considerable number of setbacks.

I can be reasonably sure that the rest of my family was thinking many of the same thoughts I was, as we lay awake for a while after the lights were out. As we listened to the strange new sounds of this house—the roof contracting in the cold and the reassuring purr of the oil burner –and we smelled the unfamiliar fragrance of stone and new concrete, I think we all realized that we had reached a new chapter in our lives. I remembered the day we first saw the preliminary drawings and I had secretly thought that, as exciting as the prospect seemed, this wonderful house would probably never materialize. But Mother and Dad had ful-filled their promise and here we were. Now that the house was a reality, what would it be like to live here?

SIXTEEN

Makeshift Accommodations

It was apparent from the beginning that life in this house was going to be complicated for a while. The next day dawned cold and clear, and we woke up in the big, cluttered space with all the windows steamed over. Tex Puth and two of his plumbers arrived early to thaw out the well pit and hook up the toilet in the children's bathroom. Dad, being well aware of Mother's priorities, began installing the kitchen cabinets and cupboards. The plumbers hooked up the water heater, which provided us with hot water by 7:30 that night. They even managed to install the water connections to one side of the kitchen sink. Nevertheless, living in the house was a lot like camping out; fun for a while, but soon you begin to miss the conveniences. It was going to be this way for a while, though, so we just had to get used to it. Looking back, it seems we were all remarkably resilient.

An unforeseen situation came up on New Year's Eve. I was almost sixteen years old, and I saw no reason why I should have to make any changes in my social calendar just because we had moved. Since we were temporarily using only the entrance to the lower level, it occurred to me that the door would not be readily apparent to most people in broad daylight, and certainly not at night. And, if you happened to be a teenage boy who was already embarrassed just to be there at all, it would be impossible. So I made a large sign, with directions on how to get to the door and posted it in the carport, hoping for the best. The sign seemed to do the job and, after visitors figured it out the first time, the next time was easy.

People had been visiting the site during all stages of the construction, and strangers had no way of knowing the house was now occupied. For a while, after we moved into the house, there wasn't much to indicate that anyone was living there, since no landscaping had been done, and construction material and workmen were still a part of the scene. Visitors continued to show up unannounced, even though getting down the driveway in the snow and ice was problematic at best. The continuing stream of sightseers was probably something we should have foreseen, but we weren't really prepared for it at the time we moved in.

Long before the move, Mother and Dad had accepted an invitation to a New Year's Day brunch, and, desperately needing a change of pace and a respite from the near-chaos in the house, they were determined to go to this party. The master suite had no working bathroom yet, and neither did the locker room; that would have to wait until Dad could build the interior wall between them. Somehow Mother and Dad managed to bathe in dishpans of water, but it couldn't have been much fun. The only consolation we had was that these makeshift accommodations would not last much longer. The morning of New Year's Day, Mother emerged from the master bathroom, clad only in her slip, and began the process of trying to locate a pair of dress shoes in one of the many boxes that were stacked in the bedroom. Something made her look up and, when she did, she found herself being regarded with some surprise by two men on horseback, just outside the bedroom window. Without a word, they looked at each other for a moment; then Mother waved—and so did the men, as they promptly turned their horses around and trotted off.

On Tuesday, the plumbers returned and, by evening, had connected the shower in the children's bathroom. Mother was really looking forward to getting us all under the shower for much-needed shampoos and scrubbing. I know she and Dad were eagerly savoring the thought of long, hot soaks under the running water. To her dismay, however, she learned that the shower drain was set in some kind of compound that required a day or two to set up properly before the shower could be used.

The absence of partitions between the children's rooms was proving to be more than an inconvenience. In May, Dad took pity on us and put up the rough walls that would serve as the core for the board and batten walls to come. They were made from salvaged boards used to construct forms for the concrete floors, which meant the walls were temporarily decorated with abstract designs rendered in dried concrete. This was an improvement, providing instant privacy, but it left a lot to be desired. There still weren't any doors to our rooms, and the bathroom door was a blanket. There were a lot of knots in the boards, with one rather good-sized one between David's and Linda's rooms. David, now eleven, worked the knot loose until it came completely out, leaving a hole about two inches in diameter. Over the hole, on his side of the board, he laboriously penciled, "Take a Peek". He was quite proud of this trick and, for a while, Linda didn't suspect a thing. I'm not sure who David thought was going to take advantage of this opportunity to steal peeks at his nine year old sister; we were a long way from being ready to entertain our friends. Linda's reaction, when she finally found out, was to stomp into her bedroom and tape a big piece of cardboard over the hole on her side, vowing to get even with David in a way he would not be likely to forget in a hurry.

Even with an occasional knothole, the temporary wall made our bedrooms much cozier, but far from soundproof. David and Linda received identical table radios for Christmas just before we moved, gifts that were enthusiastically received, since each could now choose whichever program he or she wanted. Back then, everyone listened to the radio; there was no television in our area yet. Favorite entertainment programs, such as Jack Benny and Fred Allen, or soap operas during the day, were tuned in week after week, but program preferences differed among family members, and David and Linda were no exception. Their rooms were almost mirror images of each other, so their beds were placed head-to-head on opposite sides of the wall. On school nights they were allowed to listen to the radio for an hour after they went to bed; the hour time-limit was strictly enforced. They mostly agreed upon what they wanted to listen to, which was fortunate because the sound of both radios came through the wall unhindered by any insulation. The evening programs were mostly a half-hour in length, which meant they could hear two before they had to turn off their radios. However, there was one night during the week when their preferences differed markedly; it was the night the second half-hour program was "Inner Sanctum". From a very early age, David had a remarkably vivid imagination. Stories that most people accepted as fiction, were often horrifying to my brother, who sometimes had a difficult time recognizing the line between real and make-believe in the stories he heard. "Inner Sanctum" was a really scary program, replete with screams, creaking doors and rattling chains. David wanted no part of it. On those nights, both David and Linda would listen to the first program of the hour, and then the conversation invariably went as follows:

David: "Let's turn off our radios now and talk for a while."
Linda: "No. Come on; we still have one more program."
David: "I'm ready to stop listening. Let's turn off our radios."
Linda: "You can turn yours off if you want to, but I'm going to listen to 'Inner Sanctum.'"

He was trapped. Even if he turned his radio off, he could still hear hers. I'm sure Frank Lloyd Wright never imagined that his economical design for these two bedrooms would lead to so much anguish.

When Dad finally built the cypress interior walls, in the spring and summer of 1951, it was a great relief. The pine boards were now covered with a layer of building paper on each side and faced with the horizontal cypress board and batten construction typical of Wright's Usonian houses. As specified, the cypress was finished with several coats of tung oil and then waxed. Now we had real walls and we soon had real doors to our rooms as well; doors you could shut and maybe even slam if the situation called for that. The blankets that had been serving as doors could be taken down and put away.

As the weather got warmer with the arrival of spring, the stonemasons were able to work with the stone again. Bob Cooper and his crew came back in May and began to build the grand staircase. Unfortunately, Dad had just experienced the first bout of what would prove to be continuing problems with his back. All that work in the quarry, lifting and quarrying heavy stone, as well as all the other super-human tasks he had set himself, was beginning to take its toll on his spinal column. He was diagnosed with slipped discs, fitted with a support belt and spent three weeks draped over a footstool at night—the only way he could sleep with any comfort. As a result, he wasn't able to contribute much to the construction of the stairway.

The stairs are built of the old limestone curbing Dad had bought from the city of Cedar Rapids; it was thick and wide enough to work quite well for our purpose. The stair treads measure 16" by 53", with risers of 4.5 inches, and there are nineteen stairs in all. Because of the short risers and wide treads, walking up and down the stairs is nearly effortless. Years later, when my children were toddlers, they loved to play on the steps because they are easy for small legs to manage. When the occasional fall occurred, the result was never the usual scary, head-over-heels tumble down the entire staircase, but a simple bump and scrape on a single step.

But it was nothing that a big hug from Grandma and a stick-on bandage, ceremoniously applied, couldn't fix.

More importantly, the stairs were kind to Mother and Dad as they began to show signs of age. There are no handrails, but the stone walls on either side of the stairs are easy to grasp for anyone uncertain about footing. The wide treads make it possible to use a cane or a walker with ease, and I have seen at least one person navigating up and down the stairs on crutches with very little effort. The rough surface of the stone provides excellent traction, making it impossible to slip, and there is no carpet on which to catch a foot. But, best of all, there is the sheer pleasure of pausing at either end of the staircase to take in the entire, majestic expanse of beautifully-laid stone walls; the long, narrow passageway with its cool darkness exploding into brightly lighted space at either end. I have never, in all these years, grown tired of that experience.

While Bob Cooper and crew were building the stairway, Dad was able to do enough carpentry to finish the storage system in the utility area. This meant that the last of the packing boxes could now be unpacked and the contents put away. Mother was finally able to find things that she had nearly given up hope of ever seeing again. The vacuum cleaner was unearthed at last and put to work. The story of Hercules cleaning out the Augean Stables came readily to mind as Mother labored to keep up with the mud that was constantly being tracked into the house by workmen and family as a result of the spring thaw in progress outside. The stone walls had accumulated a fair amount of concrete dust and insect carcasses during the construction process, and they needed attention as well. When Wright first proposed stone walls inside the house, Mother, thinking of the dust and spider webs that would inevitably collect there, asked him, "How will I keep all those nooks and crannies clean?'

"Oh," he said, helpfully, "just vacuum up as high as you can reach. No one will be able to see any farther than that."

Once the stairway was finished, our lives were much easier. The living room was still boarded off from the rest of the house, but the trip from one level to the other no longer had to be made using the dark and cramped wooden stairway from the locker room to the utility area. It also meant that Dad, once he was feeling better, could go ahead and begin laying the flagstone floor of the entrance loggia. He had done some simple flagstone work on the front stoop of the little brown house, but that was the extent of his experience in the medium. The loggia floor was a considerably more ambitious project; however, he learned as he worked, and the resulting floor was more than satisfactory.

Laying a flagstone floor is a bit like putting together a jigsaw puzzle, except the pieces are a lot heavier! You need to get a good balance of large and small pieces, a pleasant combination of color, and the stones must be level once they are in place. It's important to remember that you are making a floor that must be comfortable to walk on and to pick stones with reasonably smooth and level surfaces. Getting the right formula for the mortar that holds the stone in place is extremely important as well. Too much, or too little, water in the mix will cause the mortar to crumble and flake off with time. When that happens (and in one or two cases it did) the only recourse is to dig it all out and start with a fresh batch.

Next we began the awesome job of cleaning up the yard around the house in preparation for the final grading of the area that would be the lawn. This involved picking up the trash and construction debris that had been accumulating all this time, relocating what was left of the stone pile and figuring out what to do with all of the stuff once we had picked it up. We sometimes speculate on the number of cigarette butts and pipe tobacco tins that were graded under when they finally got to the landscaping. Nearly all of the men smoked, so there must have been an impressive collection. We all helped to clean up the yard—some more than others—but I'm sure most of it was done by Mother and Dad.

The driveway, at this stage, was little more than a long, badly-rutted, dirt track leading from the end of the road, where the little brown house was, down to the new house. The ruts froze during the winter months, and snow and ice filled the trenches in between. No one plowed it; it would have been a daunting task. Navigating the driveway in winter was not for the faint-hearted, but nearly everyone in Iowa knows how to drive on snow and ice, and those who needed to get to our house managed well enough. The exception, however, was teen-age boys. It's amazing that I had any dates at all during the winter months; those who had cars invariably became hopelessly stuck in the snow when they delivered me to my doorway at the end of an evening. My poor father, bad back and all, pulled them out with the Jeep, acknowledging their profuse and grateful thanks with a wry smile. In spring, it was another matter entirely. All the frozen ruts, the snow and ice, turned to a bottomless slough of rich, oozy, black mud. If dating was a problem before, it was worse now. Not only did my dates get stuck in the mud, but they ruined their carefully-tended white buck shoes and besmirched their chino pant legs every time they got out of the car to survey the situation. I doubt if anyone, with the exception of my husband, would be willing to do that for me today!

Dad took a three week vacation from the radio station at the end of May and, taking advantage of the uninterrupted work time, he accomplished a great deal. We definitely needed more furniture, so Dad agreed to try his hand at building it. Frank Lloyd Wright believed that architecture did not stop once you entered a house; he felt strongly that the interior was a major part of the whole design. To that end, he designed a large part of the furniture that would go into his houses, and I believe he was justified in doing so. One has only to look at photographs of Wright houses where the owners' individual tastes in interior design are in marked contrast to his. The effect can be compared to chalk screeching on a blackboard. Sometimes, however, Wright's clients found it necessary to draw the line somewhere along the way and to exercise some degree of their own personal taste and judgment. Some found his furniture to be more fanciful than functional.

As in many of Wright's houses, a lot of the furniture for the Grant house is built in: desks, bookshelves, benches and window seats. The chair and table designs were still waiting to be built and, as his schedule permitted, Dad began to work on some of them. One of the lovelier pieces is the table/desk in the master bedroom; another is a coffee table in the living room. Both are elegant, yet made of simple material (wood and plywood) from a reasonably simple design that Wright thought would be easy for a layman to build.

The chairs were another story. Having made the dining room table, Dad turned his attention to the seating for it. He approached the job with a certain amount of wariness because the design was markedly different from anything he had encountered up to now. Dad was not a cabinet maker, but as with everything else, he learned as he went. The chairs were semi-circular at the bottom, with slats that extended above the seats to form another semi-circle that came about halfway up an adult human back. Dad tackled the project with determination and soon had a chair finished to the point where we could all try it out. We wanted to like the chair but, even with an improvised cushion, it was really uncomfortable; there was no use pretending otherwise. The chair back provided no support (we could just imagine Wright saying how good it was for our posture), and it was hard to believe we would spend any time sitting there. Apparently, Wright did not encourage any lingering at the table. Also, the chair's seating area was quite small. Anyone with a substantial girth would not find it easy to sit down in it and, after a hearty meal, might not be able to leave it without assistance, either. The consensus was not favorable, and production of the dining room chairs came to a halt. We eventually settled on chairs of a contemporary Swedish design that we thought were compatible with Wright's table, and were much more comfortable.

Next, Dad made screens for the balcony doors upstairs, which meant that we could open our bedroom doors once the days began to get warm enough to do so. Much has been made about Wright's aversion to window screens. He didn't really believe in them, and didn't specify them for our house. He scoffed at the idea of bugs coming into the house and suggested spraying pesticide if it was a problem. Dad and Mother had other ideas. They were well acquainted with the resident population of flies, mosquitoes, gnats, wasps and bees; even an occasional confused bird sometimes ended up in the house. Frank Lloyd Wright or not, we would have screens.

SEVENTEEN

A Lot Closer to Nature

During the late spring of 1951, the big, single-pane, fixed-glass panels in the living room were finally shipped and ready for installation. Some of them were extremely large, measuring eight feet square, and the thought of someone lifting them and fitting each one into its designated place was more than a little intimidating. That job fell to the glazers, the specialists who install glass, and we had a healthy respect for the work they did.

It seemed, however, that the glazer we got, Mr. Slotsky, had a somewhat cavalier attitude toward his job. He had been recommended by the company where Dad purchased the glass, so, presumably, he knew what he was doing. But it soon became obvious that he was either showing off for our benefit, had the self confidence of someone who is not worried about losing his job, or had more than the average supply of poor judgment. He handled those huge panes of glass considerably more casually than Mother thought was necessary; and he did, in fact, succeed in breaking one because of simple carelessness. The glass for the Grant house represented a huge order for the company, and much of it was back ordered a lot of the time. A broken panel meant more delay,

Installing the big plate glass panes in the living room.

and it also meant that we had to pay for it twice. Mother lived in fear that he would break another one every time he picked up a sheet of glass, and she watched him carefully the entire time he worked. I'm sure Mr. Slotsky could not have known what a mistake it was to arouse my mother's suspicions. She was a generous person, who was happy to give encouragement to anyone genuinely trying to perform his job well. But she had no tolerance for those who didn't take their work seriously, especially when she was paying! Not only did she question his ability to do this job, but he was being paid handsomely at an hourly rate, and she was determined to make sure he earned every penny. Just as he reached the halfway point in the glass installation, in an extraordinary demonstration of bad timing, he decided to take time off for a vacation. This was a critical stage in the construction and his absence meant that much of the work schedule would be delayed until his return. As if all this wasn't annoying enough, for reasons known only to him, Mr. Slotsky sent repeated telegrams from wherever he was, asking Dad to wire him money. I can still hear Mother's reaction!

The spring rains had brought the unwelcome news that the concrete slab roof was leaking in places. The worst of the leaks was coming through the ceiling in David's bedroom, and there were an impressive number of pots and pans distributed around the room to catch the drips. Dad had roofers out to look at the problem; the first of many roofers to come. Each time they came, they tried something new; and each time they left, they assured Dad they had fixed the problem. The roof problems would continue for many years; and, as water-proofing methods and roofing technology evolved, Dad would try them all. In time he began to believe he would have to accept a simple truth: a flat concrete roof may not be a viable concept in the Snow Belt. If you are determined to have one, you must first understand that practicality has been sacrificed for aesthetics, and then you must learn to live with the certainty that there may always be leaks.

My brother, David, recently told me that most of the expensive waterproofing "solutions" might have been unnecessary. He says that, for all those years, they were trying to solve a problem that didn't exist. A few years before Dad's death, he and David began to suspect that maybe waterproofing was not the entire problem. When David went up on the roof to investigate, he discovered that no counter-flashing had ever been installed around any of the chimneys, so water was running down the uneven stone surface of the chimneys every time there was a hard rain and when the snow melted in the spring. But, instead of running down the chimney and into the house, the water was seeping back between the layers of insulation and the concrete slab where, inevitably, it came through any cracks in the ceiling that were already there. Once the flashing was done properly, the leaks stopped. If only Dad had known that from the beginning it would have saved him a lot of time, money and worry. Did he mention the problem to anyone at Taliesin over the years? If so, surely someone there would have suggested that faulty flashing might be the culprit, because, apparently, it had happened in other Wright houses. Was counter-flashing indicated in the working drawings? David says he hasn't been able to find any. I don't have answers to these questions, but I do know that a consistently leaking roof was part of a list of problems with the house that was, in time, to grow to proportions that began to change the way Mother and Dad viewed their house. It's sad to think that this problem, at least, could have been averted.

Finally, Dad began work on the flagstone floor for the living room. With the windows and doors in place, we now had a space enclosed by glass, not plywood; however, it wasn't much use to us without anything but a very rough concrete sub-floor. As the flagstone floor began to take shape, we became excited about all the possibilities for that great open room. Mother was ready to do some entertaining, now that summer was here and the tall doors (with screens of Dad's design) in the living room were open to the breezes. As soon as there was enough floor laid to accommodate a few chairs, Mother and Dad had a party. The presence of a mortar-encrusted cement mixer in the living room was only a momentary deterrent to Mother's plans. Just before the guests were due to arrive, she snatched up a pot of Grape Ivy, set it on top of the cement mixer, and arranged the vine to drape artistically down the front of the machine. The party was a great success; most of the guests had not seen the house since we moved in and were appropriately impressed by all that had been accomplished. The seating was makeshift, and there weren't enough tables to hold individual drink glasses, but the conversation was lively and, to everyone's delight, Mother provided an excellent dinner from her Frank Lloyd Wright kitchen.

Dad's work on the living room floor was progressing slowly, however, since his time to work on it was limited to evenings and weekends. He began the floor at the point where it met the steps to the dining room, and he proceeded to fill in the center of the floor first, leaving the edges until last. The north and south sections of the floor would eventually be continued outside the living room to become the north and south terraces; therefore, many of the big stones would have to be laid under the door thresholds. Until he laid those stones, however, there were sizeable spaces under each of the doors. One Sunday afternoon I was reading in the living room, awaiting the arrival of a friend. Hearing the doorbell, I started to make my way to the stairway when my attention was diverted by the presence of a big, black snake slithering slowly across the floor toward me. I immediately began shrieking,

"Snake, snake," at the top of my lungs, and I streaked up the stairs just as my friend walked into the house. In the meantime, Dad had rushed into the living room and was trying to coax the snake into a bucket with the broom, which proved to be totally ineffectual. This particular friend was a calm and practical young man who was not intimidated easily. Quickly assessing the situation, he immediately took charge. He strode up to the snake, seized it by the tail and, stepping outside, whirled the surprised reptile in the air around his head and sent it flying deep into the woods. After that memorable incident, Dad saw to it that the cracks under the doors were adequately blocked against "critters" until he could finish laying the stone.

We were still living with several raw, unpainted concrete surfaces. The specifications called for the ceilings, balcony and roof facia to be painted a light, warm beige color, but there hadn't been time to do that before we moved into the house. When the weather was warm enough to open the windows and doors, Dad began the painting job. Instead of a smooth painted surface, Wright wanted the paint to have texture. His idea for achieving texture was to apply the paint and then, while it was still wet, blow sand into the surface. I doubt if that suggestion was greeted with much enthusiasm by either of my parents, and I think that Mother didn't spend a lot of time considering it, in view of the amount of clean-up she knew would be required. Instead, Dad, using one of his favorite expressions, chose to regard Wright's idea as one that "seemed like a good idea at the time". The required texture was produced by mixing sand directly into the paint before it was applied.

That summer we discovered we were a lot closer to Nature here than we had ever been in the little brown house. The house's many doors were open almost all of the time during warm weather and, despite Dad's screens, flying insects invariably found ways in. The whine of a mosquito, just as you are drifting off to sleep, is sheer torture. We also seemed to have spiders larger than any we had ever seen before. It had been explained to us many times that spiders would not hurt us and, in fact, were our friends because they ate so many bugs. Nevertheless, it was still extremely unpleasant to encounter a big spider, the size of a salad plate, on the bedroom wall just as you were getting into bed. We wondered, anxiously, if the spider understood the part about restricting its diet to bugs.

We were living in a house so integral to the land and sky around it that thunderstorms were no longer just events we avoided by staying inside until they were over. We now learned to experience every dimension of a storm, appreciating its beauty but respecting its awesome power. We really had no choice; there were very few places to hide! Iowa is famous for its summer thunderstorms. They tend to occur when the day has been stiflingly hot and a change in the weather is coming. By day, the great thunderheads build up higher and higher until they nearly fill the sky, and the little sunlight that is left turns into an eerie yellow-green. The birds sense that something is coming; they grow silent and look for shelter. If the storm comes at night, you awaken to the rumbling of far-off thunder, which is soon accompanied by distant flashes of lightening. Gradually, the thunder and lightening grow louder and brighter, the intervals between the two are closer and closer until the entire storm is upon you and, like it or not, you are a spectator at a fireworks display of awesome proportions. When the clouds let go of their heavy load, the rain descends with a great roar. The rain immediately brings forth the pungent smell of green vegetation and newly-wet earth, one of the most fragrant scents in all of nature. If wind is part of the storm, which happens more often than not, it is sometimes so strong that it blows the rain sideways. The sound of tree limbs cracking and falling to the ground adds punctuation to this spectacular sound and light show; but the storms seldom last long. After they have moved on, all is quiet again, with only the drips from the roof drains to break the silence.

It did seem that a lot of the storms came up during the night, when we were all asleep. Our bedrooms faced south, the direction from which the summer storms often came, so, despite the wide overhanging roof, the rain blew straight into our rooms, soaking everything if we didn't get our doors shut in time. There was an unwritten drill during thunderstorms: as soon as the thunder woke you up you were supposed to get out of bed and shut your doors. But there was always the possibility that it would blow over without raining, or there would be no wind involved. You didn't want to shut your doors unless you really had to; the room would be uncomfortably hot with all of them closed. On the other hand, you couldn't wait too long. If the wind and rain started before you got out onto the balcony to shut the doors, you got soaked. Also, there was no guarantee you would even wake up in time. So it was not unusual to hear Dad out on the balcony, frantically slamming our doors shut from the outside as the storm raged away, drenching him to the skin. But it was usually much cooler the next day.

Before the summer was over, Dad finished the living room floor and started work on the south terrace floor and the curved wall around it. Mother did much of the work on the south terrace wall, and she became quite good at it. Next, Dad started laying the stone facing on the exterior of the lower living room wall and the north terrace wall. These walls, at the western end of the house, were still bare concrete which had been poured back in the fall of '49, when the footings for the living room were done. David was now old enough to help Dad work on the facing, and he put in many hours trying hard to make his stonework match what had already been done. During one of her visits, Grandma Grant sat outside and entertained David with stories and conversation to help pass the time. He found that laying stone could become boring after a while, so good company was always welcome. As fall approached, Dad finished the north terrace walls and laid the flagstone floor inside them.

We were all looking forward to spending our second winter in the house, now that we had an enclosed living room and a stairway to take us there. There would be no sheets of plywood walling off the living room and no more tarpaulins rigged up to keep out the drafts. We would have big, roaring fires in the giant living room fireplace; and we would be cozy and warm inside, while the winter storms raged without. Perhaps we were a bit too naïve.

The first hint that our expectations might be a little too optimistic came late that fall. I was downstairs after dinner, conjugating French verbs at the dining room table. A storm had been brewing all afternoon, and now it had turned into a howling gale. I have never liked wind storms, and the ominous sounds being made by the big living room windows at the northwest corner were making me nervous. The corner windows consisted of two fixed panes of quarter inch thick glass, beveled at the edges where they met. Installed properly, they were meant to withstand the strongest winds. When Dad came downstairs and passed through the dining room, I said, anxiously, "This wind's blowing really hard and the windows in the corner are making a funny noise. Do you think they're going to break?"

"Oh, no," he replied, easily. "They're in there pretty well. I'm sure they'll be fine."

I went back to my French, but I was not reassured. Sure enough,

Living room window blown out in a windstorm.

about twenty minutes later, there was a loud cracking noise, followed by the sound of glass breaking. The wind was now rushing into the room with great force. I ran upstairs, yelling, "The window blew out!"

But Dad was already coming with a tarpaulin and clamps, climbing a ladder to stop up the hole as best he could. David was there to help him, but the rest of us stayed well away. Mother forbade us to go anywhere near the windows, even though the glass had blown out, not in; but we had plenty to keep us busy, trying to deal with the mess the wind was making in the living room. Soon, Dad was able to cobble together a makeshift patch for the big hole, and the storm blew itself out with no further damage to the windows. It was not until some time later that it occurred to me to wonder why Dad had all that material at the ready if he was so sure the window was going to be all right.

The huge plates of glass were eight feet square, and everyone but Wright thought they were too big. Many people along the way tried to talk Dad out of making them that large, including Bob Cooper, but Dad held out; he thought that reducing the size would compromise the look of the great window walls. When the broken window was replaced, the glazer (not Mr. Slotsky this time!) told Dad that the glass panel had been improperly installed the first time. Apparently, the wrong type of putty had been used, or the sheet lead stripping on which the large glass panels rested was applied incorrectly, and the glass was too rigidly installed. In his opinion, the glass should have been able to withstand the pressure if it had been allowed to "breathe", or move in and out slightly with the wind. In reality, the glass should probably have been half-inch plate. True or not, the great panes of glass subsequently held through many years of howling wind storms. However, Mother was never really comfortable after that one disastrous evening. Whenever the wind blew hard she refused to sit in the room, preferring to be as far away as possible from that end of the house; the concept of those great panes "breathing" was more than she was prepared to experience at close quarters. Wright, who had originally intended the corner glass to be installed with no support at the beveled seam, relented somewhat to pressure from Dad and designed metal clips to be placed at intervals along the seam. That seemed to work well enough but, after Wright's death, Dad finally gave in and had the eight foot panels divided into three sections by the addition of two more steel mullions on each of the three sides of the glass window walls. Now the windows are well protected from storms, but the living room walls no longer resemble quite the same "curtain of glass".

EIGHTEEN

Winter in the House

The wide roof overhang was intended to serve as a screen from the sun during the summer months when the sun is high in the sky. When winter days were clear, and the sun was lower, it shone into the house unshaded by the eaves, thus providing a certain degree of solar heating. This worked well, up to a point. In summer, the house stayed reasonably cool, due to the combination of roof shade, thick stone walls and open ventilation. In winter, the direct sun could make the indoor temperature quite warm—at times during the day, uncomfortably warm.

Now, as fall turned to winter, the temperature outside became cold enough to warrant firing up the furnace to heat the floors. There is nothing quite like getting out of bed on a bitterly cold morning and putting your bare feet on a warm floor. Wright's Gravity Heating worked perfectly well throughout the part of the house we occupied during the previous winter. We had been comfortably warm then, but the living room had been boarded off from the rest of the house. Now it was time to see if Wright's concept was equal to the task of heating that enormous room after the sun went down at night.

As the weather became colder, however, and the winter winds began to blow in earnest, it became uncomfortably clear that the heating system was inadequate to the demands of the big room, with its 15 foot ceiling and vast expanses of single-pane plate glass. At first Dad and Mother put up a brave front, pointing out how pleasant it was on a sunny day and building large fires in the fireplace in the evening. However, the stark reality of the situation was inescapable; it was cold in there. The fireplace made a small difference; it was wonderfully warm in front of the fire but, once you left the fire's warmth and ventured farther into the room, your teeth began to chatter with the cold. One by one, we all began to desert the living room in the evening, either staying in our bedrooms, or sitting around the dining room table, talking or studying. Once Mother was finished with her after-dinner kitchen work, she retreated to the warmth and quiet of the master bedroom. Dad held out the longest, sitting out there reading, bundled up in several layers of sweaters and wearing gloves. After a time, however, even he gave up and began to accept the disappointing truth that we had built a beautiful room that was going to be unusable four or five months of the year if we didn't solve the heating problem.

Many of Wright's clients—those who lived in the north—experienced the same difficulty with cold houses in the winter. In his Autobiography, Wright recounts how his friend and client, Lloyd Lewis, complained of the cold during the first winter in the new house Wright had designed for him in Libertyville, Illinois,

> "So, up there off the ground, the beautiful river landscape coming in through three sides of the wide spreading house and the woods showing beneath, it was hard to keep Lloyd warm in winter. Kathryn, his wife, didn't cool off so readily as Lloyd did, but the sixty-five degrees we set for normal in a floor-heated Usonian house just didn't jibe by about twenty degrees with the Daily News

office where Lloyd worked as editor. And there was something the matter with the boiler pump there which we went down to fix or else the house would have risen to seventy-five ... I went and got it fixed but he would have been better off at sixty-five.

"... There was nothing left to do, since I had made the house part of the landscape and the landscape all around it came in on three sides (and underneath as well) but put on some double windows at Lloyd's expense just like the other folks in hiding around there do." [24]

How cold did the Grant living room get during the winter months? On the coldest mornings we came downstairs to find a thick layer of frost on the inside of most of the windows. During the day, the ice on the west and north windows never melted, but as the sun began to shine on the south windows, the resulting melt ran down the glass and onto the floor where it collected in puddles that had to be mopped up. This was annoying to be sure, but worse still was the fact that the water was soaking and staining the window frames to the extent that Dad was worried they would eventually begin to rot. He rigged up temporary devices to try and divert the water running down the panes directly onto the floor, but they were never totally successful and were a visual disaster.

David recently reminded me that the problem with the Grant heating system was not a simple matter of adjusting the boiler temperature. If we wanted to get the living room warm enough to be bearable, the water temperature had to be turned up so high that the floors in other parts of the house were uncomfortably hot. The floor in the children's bathroom became so hot at one time that we couldn't stand at the lavatory without burning our feet. As a result, Mother put a carpet on the floor, which wasn't very attractive, but at least we could brush our teeth without hopping from one foot to the other.

As a result of numerous consultations with John Hill, the consensus at Taliesin was that heavy drapes on all three window-walls would go a long way toward insulating the room from the drafts of cold air that were making the room uninhabitable. Mother and Dad estimated that it would take about 150 square yards of fabric to make drapes for that vast expanse of glass. Hanging them could be accomplished by welding the drapery rods to the exposed horizontal steel mullions, but where would they ever find material that was wide enough to meet their requirements? And, providing they could find the fabric, was it likely to be prohibitively expensive? Even if it somehow turned out to be affordable, who would they find to make the drapes?

Someone called their attention to the Bemis Bagging Company in St. Louis, a company that made commercial bagging largely for agricultural purposes. Dad wrote to them, requesting samples of the fabric they used, and asked if they would be willing to sell him the amount he needed. They readily agreed to the proposition, and quoted a price that seemed reasonable. In its natural state, the heavy cotton fabric was a light tan color with small flecks of black. Dad sent a sample to John Hill, who replied on February 4, 1952,

"The cotton material looks good. A soft ochre or gold would give it more quality. Any colors you use in the house should be subdued and at the same time warm enough to balance the stone-grey; anything from tawny gold to tan and not too dark. Give the drapes a wide hem at the height of the base piece on the sash ..." [25]

Now, having found their source, who would make the drapes? There was never any real question, of course. When the fabric had been dyed and delivered and the Singer sewing machine set up in the living room, Mother (soon to be dubbed "Jackie the Tentmaker") surrounded by 150 square yards of tawny gold Bemis bagging, embarked upon the awesome task of insulating the living room.

It took several months to make all of the drapes and get them hung. Because the fabric was so thick it was difficult to work with, and Mother broke a lot of sewing machine needles. The combined bulk of all that fabric was a problem in itself because of the amount of space it occupied. Imagine the length of one and one-half football fields in draperies piled up in your living room! The completed drapes were heavy and cumbersome to handle, so it was not easy to get them hung on the rods. But, when they were finally in place, they looked magnificent! The rich, tawny gold color suffused the room with light and gave a perception, at least, of the warmth it had been lacking. Mother had discovered that her houseplants flourished in the brightly lighted living room; we may not have been comfortable in the cold room, but plants appeared to love it. She had a very large Hibiscus bush in a planter Dad made for it, which produced a spectacular display of large, double, golden blooms every year. As chance would have it, the flowers were a perfect match for the drapes.

Did the drapery solve the heating problem? It certainly helped cut the drafts that came from the glass window-wall, but it also cut down on the amount of sunlight that came into the room. As a result, Dad and Mother found it necessary to monitor the weather conditions, adjusting the drapes to receive the maximum benefit from them. But the room was still cold, especially at night. After more consultation with the Taliesin group, another idea was suggested. Desperate for any solution to the problem, Dad employed our plumber, Tex Puth, to cut into the heating coil at the far end of the room and install a fin, or cove-type radiator under the open-fronted benches that ran along the wall at that end. The thinking was that this would increase the amount of radiation and, thus, boost the overall heating effect.

But that didn't really work, either. At some point during the following years, desperately hoping to find something that would help solve the problem, Dad experimented with one thing after another. He tried replacing the forced water radiators with electric heating coils. They put out a little more heat, but they were expensive to operate and extremely unattractive. Various valves were installed, at one time or another, in an attempt to adjust the water temperature, but nothing worked. Finally, in 1971, the furnace was changed from an oil burner to one fueled by natural gas. This brought about a significant reduction in the cost of fuel, but the monthly heating bill was still a hefty one because of the load the heating coils placed on the electrical system. The problem has never really been solved.

Herbert and Katherine Jacobs, in their book, *Building with Frank Lloyd Wright,* detail the problems they encountered with the then still experimental Gravity Heating system in the first house Wright designed for them in Wisconsin—the very first Usonian house:

> "... I should point out that sweaters and a roaring fire in very cold weather were a tradeoff that we gladly paid in exchange for year-round delight to the eye of the glass walls of the living room and bedroom, and for the lower cost of a small heating system. And we were young, buoyant and active. Had we been old we doubtless would have been uncomfortable at times." [26]

One is tempted to wonder if some of the Usonian houses, particularly those on two levels, were ever practical in areas with cold winter temperatures. At the time most of them were built, heating system technology hadn't yet caught up with the demands being placed on it by Gravity Heating during the winter months; at least my parents found that to be true. To heat a house with large open areas, many surrounded by window-walls of glass, is asking a great deal even today. Not only is it difficult to accomplish, it is becoming increasingly more difficult to afford, given the rising prices of fuel oil and gas. Who could have predicted, back in the 1940s and l950s, that the cost of heating some of the Usonian houses would put them well out of the range of middle-income families.

My husband and I live in New Hampshire, in a beautiful two-level house that was designed for us by Robert Huit Hunter—an architect who greatly admired Wright's work and who incorporated many of Wright's architectural principles into his own designs. The house is built of native stone and oak; it has glass window-walls on three sides that afford us breathtaking views of the birch woods and meadows all around us. We have an extremely sophisticated German heating system that circulates hot water through the floors and is regulated by the temperature outdoors (it has its own laptop computer!). Usually we are comfortably warm in winter, even though we keep our thermostat set below seventy degrees. But, when the winter winds blow down on us from the north and east, it can be quite cold on that side of the house, particularly when the sun is not shining. Interestingly, our local residential building code requires that spaces with as much glass as we have must have a supplemental heating source—in our case, baseboard units—which can be switched on when the house is too cold. What would Wright have thought about that? I expect he would have scoffed at the idea and pointed out that the view we are getting as a result of all that glass is well worth a little discomfort at times. And, besides, people are much healthier when they live in cool houses!

The Grant family was only uncomfortable in the winter, though. During the warmer months, we forgot about how cold it could be in the living room. We used the entire house and we loved living there. Dad and Mother had lots of parties, and we had many more visits from our various aunts, uncles and cousins than had formerly been the case when we were all piled up together in the little brown house. We were proud of our house and we loved sharing it with others. But there were limits to our tolerance.

Although there was very little publicity about the Grant house at that time, its existence was known among those who were interested in seeing Wright's work at first hand; architects, students of architecture and confirmed devotees of Wright.

One day a taxi drove down the driveway and, when Mother greeted the man who had arrived in it, he told her he was an architect from White Plains, New York. He had recently been visiting Wright at Taliesin and, during their conversation, Wright told him he should go and see the Grant house in Cedar Rapids to get an idea of the kind of stone construction he, Wright, was talking about. So the New Yorker had promptly booked a flight, and here he was. Mother gave him a warm welcome and drove him back to the airport when he left. Fortunately there were few other unannounced visitors at this point; the house was located far from town and it was difficult to find. Because it could only be reached by driving down a long driveway at the end of a dead-end road, we never had people driving by just to satisfy their curiosity. Anyone who wanted to see it usually needed to telephone first to ask for directions. Mother and Dad were always gracious about giving permission to visit the house, and usually enjoyed showing visitors around; in fact, David and I could give the tour when necessary. But we valued our privacy and, on occasion, our hospitality was strained.

One weekend afternoon, as we were finishing lunch, we were startled to see a small group of strangers walking around the house, taking photographs and peering into the windows. Giving them the benefit of the doubt, it's possible they hadn't known the house was occupied, but they did now. It was extremely rare for my father to lose his temper, but he was close to it when he stepped out onto the south terrace and said, "May I help you?"

"Oh, that's all right," one man said. "We heard there was a Frank Lloyd Wright house here and we wanted to see it. You the owner?"

"Well," Dad said, "We live here, and we don't enjoy having people wandering around our property without asking us first. I'd rather you didn't take photographs of the house, either."

"Oh, sorry. We won't stay long; we just wanted to have a look. Say, do you think we could see the inside of the house as long as we're here?"

David, Linda and I were beginning to enjoy this by now, and we were eagerly waiting to see what Dad would do next. But, if we thought Dad was going to give this guy the bum's rush, we were disappointed. He simply asked the man to leave, and to leave now. As the group got into their car and drove up the driveway, Mother said, "Maybe we should think about building a gate."

But they never did.

Dad was sensitive about photos of the house and, during the fifties he discouraged photographers from taking pictures of the house on the grounds that it was not yet finished and would be judged unfavorably as a result. For this reason, there are very few photos of the Grant house today, save those we took ourselves. In recent years, my brother has given permission to one or two professionals to photograph the house, and the results are truly spectacular. But, to this date, the Grant house has never appeared on any wall calendars illustrating Wright's work, and in very few books devoted to his architecture.

We learned to accept the cold living room, the leaking roof, the scary windows and the rude visitors as part of the adaptation process. At that point in our adventure with our Frank Lloyd Wright house, our family was still young. We kids thought it was exciting, and Mother and Dad were still hopeful that these were momentary obstacles that would be overcome with time, money, patience and hard work.

NINETEEN

Fighting a Battle

When Dad realized, back in 1945, that he wanted to build a house designed by Frank Lloyd Wright, he decided to let nothing stand in his way. He and Mother overcame more than their share of obstacles that must have seemed insurmountable at the time, but they accomplished what they set out to do. What gave him the courage to pursue this dream, or to conceive of it in the first place? Anyone who knew him well knew the answer to that question. My father was my idol and my role model as I was growing up. He taught me the importance of reading to learn, and made me understand that the need to learn never stops. He also taught me this: if you want something badly enough, and you are pretty sure you're right, you should go after it, no matter how difficult it turns out to be.

By the summer of 1953, many different activities competed for our time. Although Dad still worked on finishing the house, his attention was largely directed elsewhere. The television industry was still in its infancy in the United States, and in many parts of the country it was just becoming a reality. Dad believed it was time to bring television to Cedar

Rapids, and he set about learning everything he could about this new broadcasting medium so he could make a sound argument for his case to the management of WMT Radio. I was working as a part-time receptionist at the radio station that summer, before I left for my freshman year at Wellesley College, and I also had the job of maintaining Dad's file on the television industry. Characteristically, Dad was doing his homework; it was an extensive file.

Dad succeeded in proving his point to the station management, and on September 30, 1953, WMT Television went on the air as a flagship affiliate of CBS Television. Dad was made Vice President in Charge of TV Operations. Since the television industry was new to our part of the country, there was virtually no pool of skilled workers to draw from, and most of the first employees of WMT-TV learned their trade on the job. For example, Dad needed a film editor, so he set about convincing Mother that, if she could learn the skills necessary to build a house, she could certainly figure out what film editors did. A few years later she stepped in to fill another vacancy, and took on a daily cooking show at the station. We used to tease her about being the "Julia Child of Eastern Iowa", but the show was enormously popular and ran for several years. With Mother's considerable cooking skills and general culinary knowledge, plus her natural warmth and ability to make others feel at ease, she soon overcame her initial shyness in front of the cameras and thoroughly enjoyed herself—as did her audience.

David went off to college, and so did Linda, leaving Mother and Dad to contemplate the reality of an empty nest. A Frank Lloyd Wright nest, to be sure, but an empty one nevertheless. For a while, we were all together again during the summer school vacations but, over time, David, Linda and I married and went our separate ways. I moved east, Linda remained in the area for a while before moving on again, and David lived far away. Eventually there were grandchildren, and all had their turn every year visiting Grandma and Grandpa.

Dad on the job at WMT-TV.

Mother and Dad had many friends, and their involvement with the community expanded to include numerous contributions of their time and expertise. Dad was no longer involved with radio—the evening news was part of the past—and, now that the management of the television station had become his primary concern, any live TV broadcasts he did were limited to special events such as election returns and occasional interviews.

Dad learned of Frank Lloyd Wright's death in April 1959 when it came in over the news wire service at the TV station; he immediately called Mother to tell her the sad news. Their communication with Taliesin had all but ceased by that time, although they followed news accounts of Wright's struggle to get the Guggenheim Museum built and the acclaim with which his design for Beth Sholom synagogue was received. They continued to entertain members of the Fellowship when the migration to and from Arizona took place every year. There were always appren-

Mother on the set of Home Fare.

tices who had never seen the house; Mother and Dad enjoyed showing them around and recounting stories about the construction process. I was shocked when I heard Wright had died; it had never occurred to me that he wouldn't live forever. As children, we had regarded him as some kind of deity, so it was extremely painful to learn that he was, in fact, mortal. I think we all felt a great sadness that he was gone. He had given us something that only he could give—the privilege of living in one of his creations—and we were proud that we had known him for the short time we did.

For the first time in their lives, Mother and Dad began to travel— mostly inside the country at first—but later to destinations abroad. They always looked forward to returning home, though, and Mother entertained many elementary school geography classes with talks about the places they had been, illustrated by slides Dad had taken. Decorative pieces they found in their travels were now displayed on the many shelves and ledges in the house, and it was fun to see what was new when we came for a visit. Mother and Dad had differing ideas about how decorative items should be displayed, and it sometimes led to quiet, but humorous, struggles. Mother was of the school that liked to see objects lined up with equal space between them; Dad, on the other hand, preferred an artistic asymmetry. After dusting, Mother would arrange items according to her preference and they would remain that way until Dad noticed them. When that happened, he would stride to the offending shelf and, wordlessly, put the items back where he thought they belonged. I could always tell who had been there last.

Eventually, in their later years, they purchased a house in southeast Texas where they spent six months of the year. Mother was no longer willing to tolerate the cold, and Dad was beginning to find the work required to maintain the house in Iowa almost more than he could manage. They never thought of their escape to a warmer climate as a defection; after all, Frank Lloyd Wright had left Wisconsin every year to spend the winter in Arizona. They found they could close down the house when they weren't there; their expenses in Texas were significantly less than the cost of heating the house in Iowa. By adding anti-freeze to the water in the heating pipes, they could shut down the boiler without worrying that the pipes would freeze and burst.

There is no question, however, that the house was becoming a formidable maintenance problem, whether they were there or not. There always seemed to be something that needed attention, and Dad no longer had the time, the stamina or the will to keep up the pace. What had been only momentary obstacles in those first years in the house, now loomed as tedious tasks that never ended. There must have been times when it seemed to them that they were fighting a battle with their house. Whether it was a battle or a test of their endurance, they must have wondered just how it had become that way and who would eventually win. Wright once said to them, "You must earn one of my houses." They had certainly done that; but the prize was beginning to take on a dimension they hadn't expected. I sometimes wonder if they ever thought of giving up the house to someone younger and more robust, with young children who would fill the house with energy and laughter; someone who wouldn't mind the cold so much. But it was always assumed that the house would remain in the family, and that one of us would come to live there one day.

By this time, however, they were fortunate to have David living next door. My brother, David, has spent most of his life intimately connected to the Grant house. As children, we had all accompanied Mother and Dad on some of the trips to Taliesin to meet with Frank Lloyd Wright. At an early age, David tagged along behind Dad as he worked on the house and he observed much of the construction process first-hand. When he was old enough, he began helping Dad and Mother build the house.

After living in the southwest for a while, David and his family returned to Cedar Rapids in 1968 and, when it became clear that he would be closely involved with the maintenance of the house, he built his own house north of the Grant house driveway, just over the crest of the hill. In later years, he and Dad discussed each detail of the many repairs and corrections that became necessary as time and weather exacted their toll on the house. Some of those jobs could be formidable. David recently told me about the time he went up on the roof to clear the drains of ice.

It must have been very early in the spring, because there had been a heavy rain the day before, but the temperature had plummeted during the night and the water on the roof was now frozen solid. It was an extremely unusual occurrence, but David knew that as soon as the sun came out it would begin to melt the ice and, since the drains underneath were blocked, the water would have nowhere to go except through the many cracks and crevices in the roof. The ice would have to come out of the drains. So, with little enthusiasm for the task before him—it was raining and there was a stiff wind blowing—he headed up a ladder to the roof with a coil of strong rope and a hose hooked up to the hot water heater.

The roof was a sheet of extremely slippery ice, and it was all he could do to stay on his feet. To make matters worse, the roof was built with a gradual decline from the center to the edges to encourage better drainage, so he was, literally, navigating a slippery slope! He somehow managed to throw a loop of the rope around one of the chimneys and make it fast; then he lashed himself to the other end. This way he was able to crawl to each of the drains and melt a big enough hole through the ice to allow the water to run through, once it started to melt. He descended from the roof with no mishaps, but it had not been a pleasant experience. Fortunately, he has never had to do that again—at least, not yet.

David gradually took over the entire task of maintaining the house and, eventually, the job of looking after Mother and Dad as they grew older and less able to manage on their own. David did all this extremely well, but it became a full-time job for him.

Some time in the late 1980s, Dad began having a series of small, at first undetected, strokes; but eventually a more serious one put him in the hospital for a few days. Mother reminded us of the amazing fact that Dad had never before been a patient in a hospital. Once home, his condition gradually deteriorated to a point where Mother could no longer look after him by herself; it was clear he now required full-time professional medical care. Soon it became necessary to move him to a nursing home; he no longer appeared to have much cognizance of where he was or who was caring for him. By extraordinary coincidence, one of the patients in the nursing home at the time Dad was admitted was one of Bob Cooper's stonemasons, Johnny Timms. Dad never realized that, and it is doubtful he even understood he was no longer at home. He died on September 24, 1996, one month before his 88th birthday.

Mother elected to stay on in the house by herself. She was in remarkably good health for a woman of 87, and she had no intention of leaving the place where she and Dad had shared so many years of hard work and single-minded purpose. She continued to amaze and astound people well into her '80s, particularly those who had enjoyed seeing her on television. It was not uncommon for people to stop her at the supermarket thirty years later to tell her how much they had enjoyed her show. One woman even went so far as to exclaim, "Didn't you used to be Jackie Grant?" Among those she amazed were her doctors. At a routine medical check-up one day, a doctor, concerned about some bruising on one arm, asked, "How did you get those bruises?'

"Oh," Mother said, "I got those splitting kindling. One of the pieces slipped as I was splitting it and it flew up and hit my arm."

"The doctor could only stammer, "Y-y-you split your own kindling?"

"Why, yes." answered Mother. "Always have."

But she was never warm enough now, no matter what the season was, and the winters were increasingly hard for her to bear. In an attempt to cut down the drafts of cold air that were coming from the living room, David began boarding it off from the dining room during the winter months; Mother had a small wood-burning stove installed in the dining room fireplace and, although it was quite ugly, it radiated an amazing amount of heat. Now, when David stepped inside the house each morning to check on Mother and see if she needed anything, he was greeted by a blast of air so hot it made him reel until he became acclimatized. We all worried that she wasn't eating very well; after Dad's death she lost interest in cooking meals. So, each time Linda came to visit her, they prepared a great variety of food, packaged it up into individual portions and put it in the freezer. David did an excellent job of looking after her, but Mother had always enjoyed the company of others and now she saw almost no one; we suspected she was lonely and bored. Linda and I begged her to consider moving to one of the new retirement communities that were being built in Cedar Rapids. She always listened to what we had to say and even agreed to look at one of them, but I think she only did so to make us feel better. It became clear that she never intended to leave the house she and Dad had built together. She couldn't let go.

I often wonder what she thought about as she walked around through the silent house. She and Dad had a very clear goal in mind, and they were willing to do whatever was necessary to attain it. They both felt the joy and exultation that came with completion of their task, and the satisfaction of knowing they had taken part in an important contribution to architectural history. Late in her life, however, on an occasion when she was upset over some minor household disaster, Mother blurted out, "I hate this house!"

I was shocked to hear her say that. But now I think she may have had conflicting emotions about the house; maybe the expectations she had built for herself were never fully realized. She and Dad worked to the point of exhaustion to make their beautiful house a reality, but in order to keep going they would have needed to conjure up a clear picture of how it would finally be. It's entirely possible that they had different pictures.

Mother's childhood was spent in an environment of deprivation; but, by exhibiting a remarkable amount of determination, she had freed herself from that environment and found a new life with a man she loved. Dad introduced her to a world unlike anything she had known before, and in time their travels took them to places both splendid and exotic. As a result of his career, she and Dad traveled all over the country—from New York City to San Francisco—where they stayed in luxurious hotels and were entertained in fine homes. Mother was introduced to celebrities of the entertainment world and, as a result of her own local celebrity as a television personality, she met a great many of the dignitaries who traveled to Cedar Rapids. Mother adapted to this life with amazing ease. She was a remarkable woman, with many talents that were finally being recognized. I think those years from the late 1950s until the early '70s were, in many ways, the most exciting years of her life. She and Dad had a wonderful life together; they shared the same values and the same goals, but they also shared a deep and unwavering love for each other.

Without that love, could Mother have shared Dad's dream for the beautiful house they wanted? Could she have contributed so much to make it possible? I don't think so.

Mother, too, had a dream, but hers may not have been the same as Dad's. She loved building the house and was extremely proud of it; living in a work of art was exhilarating, but it was far from luxurious. She had not anticipated the constant worries with leaking roofs, the cold living room, the large expanses of glass that might blow out in a high wind, and the stone walls that always seemed to harbor dust and spider webs. The worries were harder for her than they were for Dad, who mostly took them in stride. For him, the never-ending problems and discomfort had always been balanced by the beauty and unique experience of living in the house. While Dad was alive, he was always able to convince her of that balance. After he was gone, it began to seem to her that the balance had tipped too far in the wrong direction. It couldn't have been easy for her to live there in those final years. The greatest job had been in the planning, the building and the heady experience of attaining the house. In the end, though, living there had become something of a disappointment for Mother.

Mother died peacefully on April 30, 2003, in the master bedroom that Frank Lloyd Wright had designed for Mr. and Mrs. Douglas Grant. She was 93 years old.

When I first began to write this book, I thought it would be easy. I had a good story to tell, and I was there while most of it was happening. But there were some aspects of the task I didn't anticipate. I knew, of course, that someday my parents would be gone and I recorded many of the discussions I had with them about their memories of Wright and their recollections of the years they spent building the house. But those conversations were more than thirty years ago; I wish I hadn't waited so long. When I finally began to write their story, there were a great many things I would have liked to ask Mother and Dad: "Why did you do it that way? How did you feel about that?" And, finally, "Was it worth it?" As I researched the book, I found a great deal of information that was new to me. I learned things that my parents were surprised to hear about, such as the existence of the previous designs that clearly were adapted by Wright to become the Grant house. Since their deaths, I've uncovered information that would have surprised them, but would have interested them very much. They were so completely occupied with building their house that they didn't have time to devote to anything that wasn't absolutely necessary to the pursuit of that end. I'm not sure they knew, for instance, that there were one or two others who were building their own Wright houses from the ground up—the Berger house in San Anselmo, California in 1950, for one. It might have been interesting for the two families to compare notes on their respective experiences, but I doubt if they knew of each other at the time. I really believe my parents thought they were unique; we certainly thought they were.

Most of all, I wish Mother and Dad were here to read this book; they would be pleased and proud to have their story told. During their lifetime, there were always people who wanted them to talk about building the house and what it was like to work with Frank Lloyd Wright. They never seemed to tire of going through it one more time.

The most difficult part of writing this book, though, has been finding a way to end the story. There doesn't seem to be a way to do that yet.

TWENTY

A Privilege Few Are Afforded

"... My Residence is of unique personal and sentimental value to me and to my family. Therefore, it is my desire that to the extent it is reasonably possible to occur, My Residence continue to serve as the residence of one of my children following my death. Although I have equal affection for each of my children, neither my daughter, Donna, nor my daughter, Linda, have resided in the Cedar Rapids area for many years, and due to their respective personal, family and business circumstances both have advised me that it is extremely unlikely that either will establish the Cedar Rapids area as her primary place of residence at any time in the future. My son, David, currently resides in the Cedar Rapids area and intends to make his home permanently in the community. Accordingly ... I hereby give, devise and bequeath ... My Residence ...to my son, David ..."

Charlotte K. Grant, Last Will and Testament, August 21, 1996

It was meant to be so simple. Everyone agreed that David should have the house. He had been looking after it for years, he knew it intimately, and now he would be able to live there. It was the way Mother and Dad had wanted it. But it has become somewhat more complicated in the years since Mother's death.

Both the city of Cedar Rapids and the adjoining town of Marion have expanded in the years since the Grant house was built. David, Linda and I own all of the land around the house for a substantial distance, and David has maintained the land so beautifully that it now resembles a magnificent, natural park. The rolling green meadows are mown on a regular basis, the woodlands are properly managed and David has built a labyrinthine network of walking paths throughout the property. It is the perfect setting for the magnificent stone structure on the knoll above. But the area surrounding the Grant property has become more developed with time, and what was once a remote, country location is now an established residential community. The dark night sky, once the backdrop for spectacular displays of aurora borealis and star constellations, is never completely dark any more. The horizon is now filled with the bright illumination of shopping centers and the blinking lights of communication towers.

None of us has gone to live there. I live in New Hampshire and Linda lives in Alaska; we couldn't be farther away and still live in the same country. David lives in the house he built across the driveway from the Grant house, even though he is the Grant who owns it now. His house is attractive and comfortable, and is the place where he raised his family. It is understandably difficult for him to move to the Grant house, although he and his family spend a considerable amount of time there.

The decision is a hard one for him to make, and is further complicated by the two houses' extreme close proximity to each other. For years it was convenient to have David living so near; he was readily available to help Dad with whatever the current project was and, when Mother and Dad were away, he could keep close watch on the house. Later, as Dad's health became steadily more worrisome, Mother felt more secure with David there. After Dad's death, Mother was really only able to remain in the house alone because of David's presence next door. Back then, no one thought to wonder what would happen when the time came for David to make the Grant house his home. If he moves there, what's to be done with his present house? If he sold or rented either house, he wouldn't want to remain next door. So far, there are no good answers. It's a complicated problem that will need a great deal of wisdom and consideration to solve.

David is doing an admirable job of restoration on the house. Anyone who has ever lived in a Wright dwelling must surely know that they require a great deal of maintenance. The Grant house is no exception; time and weather have left their marks and, the job of restoring the house to something near its original condition is a major one. David is currently working on rebuilding the walls of the north terrace, a job that made it necessary for him to re-open the old quarry and dig out enough stone to use in the wall. I expect that laying stone again has brought back all sorts of memories of the days when he was working on the original wall and Grandma Grant read him stories while he worked. It's nostalgic to think so, of course, but David was eleven then; now he is seventy and he is doing most of it alone.

In his book, *The Natural House,* Frank Lloyd Wright said,

> "…When you are conscious that the house is right and is honestly becoming to you, and feel you are living in it beautifully, you need no longer be concerned about it. It is no tax upon your conduct, nor a nag upon your self-respect, because it is featuring you as you like to see yourself." [27]

When Wright conceived his Usonian house design for middle-income families, he could easily have been thinking of my parents. The site was perfectly suited to the design, the abundance of beautiful, natural stone easily met the requirement for good building material and, by doing a great deal of the work themselves, my parents were able to build the house at a considerably lower cost than would otherwise have been the case. The flaw in this ideal arrangement of circumstances didn't begin to surface until many years had passed. Buildings and people age with time and, similarly, the cost of repairing both increases significantly. When things first began to go wrong with the house, it was an annoyance to be dealt with. The roof that leaked and the cold living room were problems for which some solution surely existed, if only the right one could be found. As the years went by, however, and Dad was less able to attend to the constant maintenance that was required, the house began to assume the role of his own, personal burden. If David hadn't been there to help, Dad and Mother might have given up trying to take on the enormous responsibility they now faced. In a sense, that's what they were doing when they began leaving the house for longer and longer periods of time. The affordable house had become a high-cost, high-maintenance cause for great concern, and it was becoming more and more difficult to live in it "beautifully". In 1979, when Dad and I were reminiscing about building the house, he said to me, "People often ask me, 'Would you do it all over again?' I guess I'd have to say, 'Probably not at this stage in our lives.'"

There is much work to be done on the house and time is passing quickly. The south terrace walls are beginning to crumble as rain is driven into the cracks, freezes and breaks the stone apart. Years of leaks in the roof have left ugly brown stains; and the scars of expansion cracks sprawl across the ceilings, providing unwelcome reminders of troublesome times in the past. The cypress woodwork, both inside and out, is badly stained and needs to be restored. The hardware for the doors and windows was improvised by Dad at the time, because no specifications were written for it and none of the stock hardware fit the narrow frames. He assumed that Wright's wealthier clients simply had appropriate hardware fabricated to fit each requirement. Mother always complained about the "hen house latch" on the main entrance door, but it is still there and is showing its age. No one of these tasks is insurmountable, of course, but when considered together they present a serious obstacle to making the house livable again. The living room is still frigid during the winter months, but it doesn't matter as long as it is rarely occupied. David thinks that new technological advances in heating systems would probably provide a solution to the problem, but it's a big commitment to make as long as the house's occupancy is in doubt.

The future of the Grant house is uncertain at this point. I know Mother and Dad had visions of the house being passed along from one generation to the next, always remaining in the family, but circumstances seem to have dictated otherwise. David, Linda and I have two children each. They are all adults, most of them live far away from Cedar Rapids, and some have children of their own. As far as I'm able to determine, none of them has expressed any interest in occupying the house.

So, for the time being, the house isn't used very often. It's difficult for me to accept that, because it's always been a significant part of our lives. So many good times were had in that house over the years. I always said I wanted to be married there, descending the grand staircase with the appropriate bridal train trailing behind me. In March 1976 I was married in front of the big living room fireplace; I didn't have a train, but that ceremony was just what I'd always had in mind.

I visited my brother two years ago, and I stayed in the house by myself for the first time in a long while. So many memories came rushing back as I wandered through the house by day and went to sleep each night in my old room. It gave me great pleasure to move the vases and figurines on the long stairway bookshelf back to the artistic asymmetry that Dad always preferred, and to run my fingers over the titles of all the books he'd read. I looked at Mother's favorite cookbooks and enjoyed the comments she often added to the margins next to the recipes she used, remembering how those dishes tasted. It is just as difficult to take a shower in the children's bathroom as it always was, and I seem to have forgotten what switches turn on which lights. But I heard the familiar call of owls in the night; I woke up to the same faint fragrance of toasting grain at the Quaker Oats plant; and, once again, the view down the long stairway made me catch my breath. It was good to be back.

When Dad wrote his first letter to Frank Lloyd Wright, back in December 1945, he started the process by which he and Mother would begin working to build, not only a house, but a new way of life. It took them a long time to accomplish it, but once they started they never looked back. Dad had a great deal of respect for Wright, and I believe the respect was mutual. Wright designed the only kind of house Dad felt was appropriate for his family; and, despite popular lore to the contrary, he and Mother always found the Great Man delightful company and quite easy to work with. At the same time, Dad was the embodiment of the client Wright had imagined for his Usonian houses and, what is more, this client was earning the house by doing all the work himself. It was, as Wright said himself, "An American Proceeding."

At the beginning of this book, I said that Wright was fond of telling his clients that living in one of his houses would change their lives. People often ask me if that was true for us. Mother and Dad spent forty-five years together in the house, years in which their lives took on dimensions they could never have predicted. They were so proud of their Wright house, and they had every reason to be proud. They took on a project so daringly bold and outrageously difficult that few thought they would bring it off, but they astonished everyone—including themselves! And by accomplishing this remarkable task, they acquired a measure of self-confidence they might otherwise not have found—a confidence that gave them the courage to make decisions that affected their careers and sent them off in directions they might never have contemplated. It all began back in 1945 when they decided to ask Wright to design a house for them. Yes, it changed their lives; it changed all our lives. We know our parents were unique and we know the house is unique. The design is Frank Lloyd Wright's but, by giving the house literally everything they had, Doug and Jackie Grant gave it life.

But was there a fatal flaw in the dream—an unexpected catch? I'm sure they never suspected in the days the house was taking shape that some-day they wouldn't be able to meet the demands it would make on them. But it seems to me now that, despite the many trials they went through to get there, and the gradual realization that the house had begun to ask more of them than they were capable of giving, they always knew that living in their Frank Lloyd Wright house was a privilege very few are afforded. On the whole, it had been a good trade-off.

As I write this narrative, the future of the Douglas Grant house is yet to be determined. I fear that deterioration will continue until the task of reversing it becomes a burden too great to bear—financially, physically and emotionally. For now, though, the house still emerges from the hill-side to soar dramatically into the air like some majestic ship's hull tower-ing above the waves. The living room may be cold, but its interior color scheme is still dictated by the changing of the seasons, and the glass window-walls shimmer with the reflected light of each sunset. It is still a splendid house—one of the best of its kind—and we had many wonder-ful years there. I wish it well for the future.

NOTES

1. Copyright Frank Lloyd Wright Foundation

2. (FLLW Foundation)

3. (FLLW Foundation)

4. Copyright Frank Lloyd Wright Foundation

5. (FLLW Foundation)

6. (FLLW Foundation)

7. Copyright, Frank Lloyd Wright Foundation

8. (FLLW Foundation)

9. Curtis Besinger, *Working with Mr. Wright: What it was Like,* Cambridge University Press, 1997, pp. 174-175.

10. John Sergeant, *Frank Lloyd Wright's Usonian Houses,* Whitney Library of Design 1976, p. 140.

11. Copyright, Frank Lloyd Wright Foundation

12. (FLLW Foundation)

13. (FLLW Foundation)

14. Bruce Brooks Pfeiffer, *Frank Lloyd Wright, the Masterworks,* Rizzoli International Publications, 1993, p. 256.

15. John Sergeant, *Frank Lloyd Wright's Usonian Houses,* Copyright 1975 John Sergeant, p. 141.

16. Scott and Helen Nearing, *Living the Good Life,* Schocken Books, New York, 1954, pp.59-69.

17. (FLLW, The Masterworks, p. 148)

18. (Besinger, p. 184)

19. (*Frank Lloyd Wright's Usonian Houses,* p. 112)

20. Frank Lloyd Wright Lecture to Taliesin Fellowship, June 4, 1950 Copyright 1950, The Frank Lloyd Wright Foundation

21. Edgar Kaufmann, Jr., *Taliesin Drawings,* Wittenborn, Schultz, Inc., 1952, p. 22.

22. Alvin Rosenbaum, *Usonia,* The Preservation Press, 1993, p. 168.

23. Frank Lloyd Wright, *The Natural House,* 1954, pp. 159-60.

24. Frank Lloyd Wright, *An Autobiography,* copyright 1977 by the Frank Lloyd Wright Foundation, pp. 522-523.

25. Copyright 1952, Frank Lloyd Wright Foundation

26. Herbert and Katherine Jacobs, *Building a House with Frank Lloyd Wright,* copyright 1978, by Herbert and Katherine Jacobs, p. 54.

27. (FLLW, *The Natural House,* p. 136)